# BE...

## THE WINNING PRESENTATION

Be Brave!

Dena

# BE....

## THE WINNING PRESENTATION

The essential handbook to master the
short list interview and win more work.

## DENA L. WYATT

Print information available on the last page.

Rev. date: 10/14/2016

**To order additional copies of this book, contact:**
Xlibris
1-888-795-4274
www.Xlibris.com
Orders@Xlibris.com
733313

# TABLE OF CONTENTS

# ACKNOWLEDGEMENTS

I dedicate this book to all of the talented, hard-working people in the construction and design industry. These dedicated people give us our roads and bridges, our high-rises, and our educational environments. They create our work and play environments, the living and healing places that restore us and our families, and, virtually, everything in-between. Thank you for choosing this profession.

Many thanks go to the visionary, creative, and inspiring people I've had the pleasure to meet and work with over the years through the Society for Marketing Professional Services. These caring, smart, and competitive people give me the energy and inspiration to BE the best.

A special thank you goes to dear friends, Stacy Stout, Marcy Loughran, and Deb Schindler. These strong, brilliant, and talented women have supported me, from day one, in so many ways. And, of course, to my family for their endless love and support.

To the many gifted people who have helped me become one of the foremost marketing trainers, coaches, and strategists in the design, construction, and real estate development industries, I extend my appreciation and gratitude. I cannot thank you enough for your belief in me and your contributions and support. Perhaps, this book is a good place to start.

# INTRODUCTION

Why This Book is…
What You Need to Win…
…*And What You Stand to Lose Without It*!

In the pages of this book you will discover how to leave your competitors behind and increase your win rate.

This book is all about how to **BE more successful** and **win more work**.

But don't worry: **You won't be asked to memorize anything**.

There are **no tests, only tips and techniques you can take away** and use tomorrow.

**In this book you will find a new, focused approach to** one of the most underestimated and feared moments in the career of architectural, engineering and construction (AEC) professionals.

## The Client Interview, aka the "Short List" Presentation

The client interview is frequently one of the most overlooked aspects of a project pursuit. While everyone sharpens their pencils on the cost estimate and works and reworks the schedule to the $n^{th}$ degree, very little time and effort is spent preparing for the one chance you have to actually meet with your prospective client and discuss their project and unique needs. It is not likely a coincidence that the interview is also the most feared aspect of the process. It is well-known that public speaking is frequently one of a person's top fears. This is particularly true of the highly-skilled technical professionals found in AEC firms. Technical design and construction professionals, generally, are not trained to present their thoughts and ideas in front of a diverse group of individuals, yet that is exactly what you need to do to win.

In the end, every firm that has been short listed and is interviewing to design or build the project is qualified. The ONLY thing you can do to affect the outcome, at this point, is to give the best presentation, one that connects with the client. Clients don't hire robots to build their projects; they hire PEOPLE. The presentation is your chance to make a connection with the client and show them that yours is the right team.

This invaluable guide was written for professionals in the design and construction industry, from project managers, designers, engineers, and superintendents to principals, executive managers, and CEOs. These are the people who prep-up, step-up and perform - in those sometimes dreaded, make-or-break, client "short list" interviews.

I've spent over 20 years coaching key players to compete for and win, the short list interview. So please enjoy and have faith: You are about to BE-come truly "evolutionary" and lead your team to success!

In this book, you will **discover the underlying purpose of the presentation.**

You will learn how to **restructure and refine the way you approach your presentations.**

To succeed, you must learn to do more than compete - **you must learn how to win.**

After you walk away with a client's next project, after you have left your competitors in the dust and are wondering how you won the job, you will know why you read this book.

For now, here's how to use it. **This book is a concise, easy-to-navigate reference guide. It is meant to be used and personalized to your situations, so please:**

**Mark it up.**

**Dog-ear the pages.**

**Fill it with "sticky-notes."**

**Look for every quick, memorable.**

**Do a quick review before EVERY Presentation.**

This is what it's for.

This book has been engineered to provide critical tips that will help you connect with clients during your next short list presentation.

## Master Your Own Mind Games

Get ready to send that worn, old carton of "success" tapes and videos to the landfill. I'm going to show you how to eradicate the mental mind games that rob you of your full potential as a winning presenter.

By absorbing the critical tips in this book, you will hone your ability to *professionally...*

**Be Yourself**
**Be Conversational**
**Be Positive**
**Be Trustworthy**
**Be Prepared**

**Be Confident**
**Be Passionate**
**Be Interesting**
**Be Memorable**

We don't need memory techniques; we just need to learn how to win. Now, while we don't need to memorize, learning takes some practice, and this book is about teaching you what and how to practice. Besides, how can you remember anything when you don't believe? How can you believe when you don't know why? I'm about to show you why.

# *Master the client presentation*

# *...and you will unlock the gateway to success and win more work.*

While it may seem easy to "be" all of these things, in the context of a presentation, it is anything but that. For instance, you can easily "**be yourself**" with friends and family. But, try it with a multi-million-dollar project on the table!

For now, take away the following tip and believe it, because it is absolutely true. Tear the tip below out of the book if you have to. Put it in your wallet or purse.

 *You have earned the right to be there! You are the expert. Relax and "BE the Expert" when you present.*

The client simply wants to get to know you!

When you reach the final chapter of this book, I'm confident you will BE just that. Your evolution has begun.

## ...Let's go to Chapter One!

# WHY AREN'T WE WINNING?
# THE NEED FOR A
# NEW APPROACH

Let's look at the stodgy and familiar old-school construction firm. They show up for the interview wearing dark, matching suits, and toting oversized photos of their impressive projects. They talk about themselves, how long they've been in business, all the great projects they've done, and the awards they've won.

Some of them even sound like professional game show hosts. However, they have failed to answer one key question:

# *What is the purpose of a client presentation?*

### Is it to impress?

### Is it to educate or inform?

### Is it to entertain?

### None of the above?

The answer IS...NONE OF THE ABOVE! (You knew that didn't you?)

Here's the answer: The winning presentation does one thing really, really well...

# *The winning presentation PERSUADES.*

You've already submitted a proposal that educated and informed them about your qualifications, capabilities, and history. If the client didn't think you were qualified to do the project, you wouldn't be at the interview.

The clients don't want a rehash of your proposal; they are more savvy and sophisticated than that!

## The Traditional "Dog and Pony Show" Approach is O-U-T!

To "persuade" your client selection committee that you and your firm are the best possible choice, it will take more than a rehash of the required pre-qualification documents.

 *They have already reviewed your SOQ, RFQ or RFP. Think deeper. Think: What Can You Do for THEM? How can you solve the challenges of the project?*

Those beautifully developed proposal documents did their job and put you in the final round; now you must take it to the next level. Now, the client wants to meet your team and see and hear more.

# *Lasting persuasion begins with emotional connection.*

### Connect EMOTIONAL dots to create persuasion

Demonstrate a deeper understanding of the client's emotional needs and concerns:

- **Show them you understand the risks of the project.**
- **Discuss how you can solve *their* challenges.**
- **Prove you've solved similar challenges.**

Have you noticed something about the items above? They aren't concerned about **you**! They aren't worried about **your** capabilities. They want to know how you are going to address what **they** are worried about.

## *...Talk about them!*

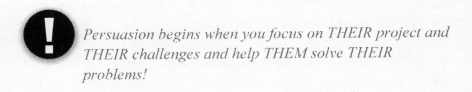

*Persuasion begins when you focus on THEIR project and THEIR challenges and help THEM solve THEIR problems!*

# Truth Time

Be honest with yourself. During your last presentation, how well did your key elements match up with theirs? Did you demonstrate successful solutions to the challenges they face? Did you give them confidence in your team?

> **Truth #1:** I'm guessing you THOUGHT you addressed their concerns. But, in reality, you did so in a generic manner that lacked the specifics and details that build trust and confidence.

> **Truth #2:** If the client had few-to-no questions...*then went with another firm*...you know what I'm thinking? I'm thinking: You didn't connect with them and they let you walk...to clear the room for the next team. (Don't we hate it when that happens?)

> **Truth #3:** When you hear just a few easy questions after your presentation or none at all ...*and you win the project...* you hit the sweet spots. You dealt with *their* challenges and concerns in your presentation, built trust and confidence and showed them you were the right team.

If Truth #3 applies to you, congratulations. Can you do it again? Can you do it every time?

We'll talk about that when we look at that fearless and cocky person who somehow thinks he can just "wing it" and win...until he goes down in flames and takes his team with him.

You know the type. Later, I'll show you what happens to our "wing it" commando. For now, suffice to say that you do not want to be his wing-man.

# What Do Clients Say About The Interview Process?

Some of you still need to be convinced, so let's hear from a recent survey of public and private clients. After we conducted this study, the following trends and comments rose to the top.

**"We did not want a 'sales' presentation. We wanted to know what *they* knew about us."**

**"The losing presentation was canned and sounded generic. The winners' presentation was totally geared towards us."**

**"The winning team had a very detailed approach, especially when it came to showing us how OUR issues would be solved."**

Notice how not even one respondent said they needed more info about the presenter or the presenter's firm?

## Just remember...

- **The traditional "Dog and Pony" approach is out!**

- **It isn't about you.**

- **Emotional connections win projects.**

- **Know what they want.**

- **Focus on *their* challenges, *their* solutions...*them, them, them*!**

...Not you.

Got it? Great! You're already working on your first, slam-dunk winning interview.

## 2

### WHY WINNERS WIN
### ATTITUDE

So, who wants to win work? Duh? *Everybody* **wants to win!** But here's the catch: **So does your competition!**

Chances are they're preparing and practicing right now, getting ready to unseat you and your team in the next interview...**EIGHT seconds** after you start.

Yes, I did say **"eight"** seconds. Hold that thought; we'll come back to it.

Back to our objective: Everybody wants their RFPs to turn into work; we know that and you can increase your win rate so more of them do become work...if you don't *melt down* during the interview.

Here's the thing about those pesky interviews: They show us "unplugged." They reveal our "human factor." Who we are, how we communicate, and what it will be like to work with us.

The client's primary concern is *who*...WHO are they going to be working with...WHO are these *people*?

Call it the client's inner owl: Who...who...whooo? YOU, that's who... if you present with the right attitude.

## The Alchemy of Attitude

This is where what I call the Alchemy of Attitude kicks in and it is, unfortunately, an inexact science. Alchemy itself was a notoriously inexact science back in Merlin's day and so it remains today.

But a positive and correct attitude can be consistently plugged into *winning techniques* to deliver reliable results. Conversely, the wrong kind of attitude can turn off your audience and send you packing.

Let's begin with having a complacent attitude when it comes to coming in second.

## Why "Second" Sucks

Winning work is actually pretty easy if you understand winning concepts.

This begins with how you think. If you think it's *"okay"* to *"do your best"* and come in second, put this book away right now because it's not for you.

…You're still reading? Great, we have a lot in common!

I've been teaching the best and brightest in our AEC community for many years and they have pretty much one thing in common: They want to get better and they want to win work. That's why they hire me.

I teach people to win multi-million-dollar presentations…NOT how to come in second.

# *This is how winners think: "IT SUCKS TO COME IN SECOND!"*

They're right. "Second" pays zip, zero, nada. As the saying goes, "Second" means first loser. I once saw a photo of a mock tombstone that read "He Tried."

Do you want to "die trying" in your next presentation? No! I'm not going to let you!

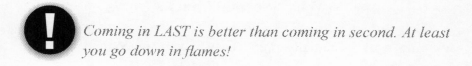

*Coming in LAST is better than coming in second. At least you go down in flames!*

## Excuses Losers Make

Chronic losers say things like: *"No wonder we lost, we're in such a crazy market."*

This is one of many catch-all clichés for coming in second, or third, or dead last. I'm not even sure what this means, other than competition is fierce and people are willing to crawl over broken glass to get the job.

Okay, we're in a crazy market. So what? Up or down, markets are always crazy because we're in one of the most competitive industries on the planet. Substitute other words for "market" and they fit anything from sports to politics.

*"We lost because we're in such a crazy season...we were (batting, racing, biking) in such crazy weather."*

Forget it. This is the language of denial. Their approach was wrong and that's it.

Okay, so maybe you lost; it happens. When it does, let's try:

*"Hey, we lost. Let's learn what went wrong, Next time, we'll change our game plan and knock it out of the park!"*

That's better and here's the GOOD NEWS: The new Game Plan is easier than you think.

**It's time to reinvent how you handle the make-or-break, under-estimated, and misunderstood client presentation.**

Right now, here's what you really need to remember:

- **Every team on the short list is equally qualified.**
- **Whether it's you, the ABC Company or the XYZ Group, you are ALL qualified.**
- **Face it, you can ALL do the job or you wouldn't be asked to interview.**

# *Today's Short List Interview is an old playing field...with a brand new playbook.*

The interview is coming. You know they're going to pit you and your competition against each other and make a decision based on what? A 30-minute interview? A 30-minute Q&A? That's precisely right. (The times may vary, but you get the point.) This is unbelievable, but true. Think about it; if they were going to make their decision just on your proposal, there would be no need for an interview. **Interviews matter.**

# *Owners base their entire project, costing multi-millions of dollars...*

# *...on a*

# *30-minute presentation!*

I know it *sounds* crazy. But that's what it comes down to and I'll tell you why in a minute.

You cannot underestimate how important it is to nail this part of the process, to win the competition and bring home the project. Weeks and months have gone into getting to know the client, completing the RFP, and yet:

- **Traditional companies still treat the final interview like any old sales pitch.**

- **Some try to wing it - like they do when shooting the breeze with their friends.**

- **Some try to be "all things to all people" and dilute their core message.**

- **Some competitors throw up their arms and pitch the old, "what-the-hell," low-dollar bailout.**

Fatalistic "low-dollar" bidders create a "lose-lose" situation for everybody, *including the client.*

Guess what? Smart clients know this. As for the contenders above: Every one of them is about to lose because, in this case...

- **Smart clients know "cheap" doesn't equate to "best" quality.**

- **Smart clients know the perils attached to low-ball estimates.**

- **Smart clients want a well-calculated price point.**

- **Mainly, smart clients want a realistic price addressing their needs and concerns.**

*Good clients look for the best, not lowest-cost, operators. They will pay IF you can show them how you will resolve their concerns.*

## The Fine Art of Not Being "Flat"

The following client-response just slays me. I mean, it's a real stinger in the marketing world:

**"The team lost because their presentation 'was flat'."**

This client went on to add terms like **"lack of enthusiasm"** and even **"lack of passion"** for the project. Passion and enthusiasm are both drawn from your attitude. As goes your attitude, so goes your presentation. Before we look at how to harness your winning attitude to show your enthusiasm and passion, let's talk about what NOT to say. Have you ever heard someone start off (and *die immediately*) with:

"I'm so excited about your project?"

Of course you have. We all have. Everybody says that.

Our goal is for you to *Show without having to Tell*. That's what it's all about, right? **Enthusiasm shows.** It's infectious. People respond to enthusiasm without you having to say a word.

**You should be able to *show that passion* and a client should be able to feel that passion. You should be able to show it *without using words* like "excited" or "passionate."**

*Passion and enthusiasm come from your attitude and show through in your voice, gestures, and facial expressions.*

Clients want a team that is as excited and passionate about their project as they are.

Let's move on and begin to learn the building blocks for game-changing presentations and what clients are really looking for.

# 3

## DOING YOUR HOMEWORK
## PLANNING AND RESEARCH

When we go in for the final pitch, we have only one task: **Convince** the client that, **WE**, without a doubt, **ARE** the team to pick.

I call it Presentation 101. This is the persuasion we talked about earlier.

AND you need to keep this key concept in mind:

# *Clients don't want perfection... they want connection.*

So how do we connect with people we don't really know? Simple, we get to know them. Before you even start worrying about what you are going to say in your presentation, you need to do your homework. The homework isn't hard, but it does take some time and effort. It isn't complicated either; you just need to learn everything you can about your client and their project.

## Know Their Business

How can you understand what they need if you don't know what they do?

# *If you understand how your client makes money, how they're going to use that building, and what success looks like to them, you're already way ahead.*

Part of achieving a comfort level for your team is to make sure that everyone understands how the CLIENT services THEIR clients. Once you demonstrate that kind of depth of understanding, they know you can build a much better building for them.

## Know Their Project

When I train presentation teams I like to ask the following question:

How many times have you driven by a client's project site, for the very first time, *on the morning of the interview*? (Come on…!)

Okay, some of you might spend a little more time: Maybe you'll drive by the site at least the day before. (I always get a chuckle or two on that one.)

Let's face it, we all get busy, things pile up at the office until – uh-oh – the presentation's tomorrow *and **we're not exactly sure where the project actually is**…*not in terms of having really studied the turf.

## *"While driving a superintendent to an interview, we drove by the site that morning…for the very first time."*

**…My own words, exactly. Yikes! …Sound familiar?**

Okay, in his defense, he was just coming off another project. He'd had no time to come into the office and practice with us. Meanwhile, the rest of us were so slammed, nobody had time to check the daily mail.

We all know how it is (especially in this *crazy* market). But, if you want to do everything you can to win, you have to dedicate the time to get it right. Here's what it takes:

- **Study the client's potential motives and needs.**
- **Gain a site-based sense of the project.**
- **Drive the neighborhood.**
- **Study the site and surrounding area, at different times of day, if possible, *FIRST HAND*!**
- **Talk to people that have worked with this client before or the users of other facilities.**

Only then, will you understand potential problems from your client's point of view. Only then, can you be ready to address solutions for the client.

In other words, you need a *mind's-eye perspective* – not a memorized script - before you step into that 30-minute presentation. The goal is not to memorize some script, but, to simply talk about what you know, just as if you were describing your last project to your family or friends.

If you don't display this level of understanding, a client will feel it in a heartbeat. So, when it comes to carving out time to tour a potential job site, ask yourself this question:

*If it takes an hour, even if it means driving a half-day to a site, how much time is it worth losing in a final interview...if you don't?*

## End of Story

You're probably wondering what happened to our poor superintendent. Well, here's the real story: After dashing past the site in my car, we went directly to the interview where he said (and I quote):

**"Well, as I drove by your site this morning, for the first time, I noticed…"**

He couldn't even say he had walked the site! Needless to say…we didn't get the job.

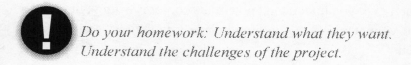 *Do your homework: Understand what they want. Understand the challenges of the project.*

## Five EASY Issues

I can tell you this about your audience: **All clients face five, basic issues**.

Understand these! Reference these and **they'll save you every time**.

## Save Me Time

Schedule means everything. You almost always find a good reason they need that building open by a certain date. Understand that and you will connect and resonate with them.

For retail clients, it's usually seasonal. The emphasis was once on Black Friday. It's more online these days but, back in the days of the brick-and-mortar retail store, if you weren't open for Black Friday, forget it. You would have missed that whole retail Christmas season.

If it's a school, the building has to be open in August before the school year begins.

Understand what is driving your client's schedule and their time frame. And, show them how you can meet it.

## Save Me Money

Has anyone been given a project with an unlimited budget? Most owners have tight budgets.

Once in a while, we run into a client who wants to spend all the money they have. If they're receiving a grant, they don't want to give any money back at the end of the day – so maybe your story of cost savings and the way you return fifty-percent cost savings at the end of the job – is not going to work with this owner. They want that money put in their project and used.

So, understand the money no matter what issues are involved.

Let them know you're aware of their budget issues and how to solve them.

## Make Me Look Good

All clients have a boss – the general public, stockholders or a user group – so they have to answer to somebody out there, don't they? Know who will be watching this project come out of the ground. Think of the people making the selection: Who do they answer to? How can you make them look good?

## Make it Easy

Our owners have a day job full of deadlines and responsibilities. Now, they have to manage this project. Show them you're easy to work with and how you will hold their hand through the process.

## Keep Me Out of Trouble

I've worked with oil and gas professionals for years, and they walk that fine line with the Environmental Protection Agency (EPA). All they want to do is stay out of trouble and hold tight to regulations without spending an arm and a leg to do so. Understand how to keep your client safe and know about regulations that might be affected.

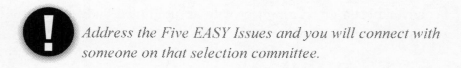

*Address the Five EASY Issues and you will connect with someone on that selection committee.*

Once you understand the challenges of the project, you can get to work on how you and your team can solve these challenges. We will talk more about how you present your solutions in a bit. But, first, let's look at what clients are looking for and just what they are thinking during these interviews.

# WHAT ARE THEY THINKING? UNDERSTANDING YOUR CLIENT

Have you ever come away from a presentation just dying to know what a client was *really* thinking? Sure, we all have. Throughout my career I've interviewed hundreds of clients after winning, and more importantly, after losing short list presentations. Time and again, these clients have said:

- **"We don't want a 'sales presentation'."**

- **"We want to know what YOU know about US."**

- **"We want to know what YOU know about OUR project."**

- **"We want to know how YOU will help...US!"**

That's it. Believe it. In the process of conducting these de-briefings on behalf of my company or my clients, I consistently ask these questions:

1. **What did they feel after watching the presentation?**
2. **What did they look for?**
3. **What stood out?**
4. **What did the winning team do well?**

5. **What set a team above the rest?**
6. **What did any team do that impressed them?**

**I've probed for SPECIFIC, scale-tipping factors.**

I kept asking until I found out what *really* caused them to go with a particular contractor or professional design team...and reject others.

I got into their heads. I learned to watch presentations through their eyes. This is what I found. The teams that connected, the teams they remembered, all had build TRUST and not only showed, but proved, to the client they could successfully deal with and solve the challenges of that project. See, at the end of the day, your clients are looking for the "SAFE CHOICE." The firm that can get it done and make them look good.

### Bye, Bye Dog-and-Ponies
We used to call it "show time" because, way back when, you just went in and did the old dog-and-pony show.

Most people like dogs. Kids love ponies. But, neither has a place in today's presentation room.

### *Speak!*
**During the tedious old dog-and-pony show, somebody gives an opening speech like this:**

*"We've been in business since 1964. We were founded on a platform of trust and integrity and are proud of the fact that 80% of our work comes from repeat ..."*

Ugh. This sounds like the human version of an old dog doing the same old trick for a tasty treat.

Blah. Blah. Blah. Years ago, clients bought it. They would scarf it down every time.

Not now.

**They won't "eat it up" anymore.**

**They don't want the standard presentation.**

**You've done your up-front work: They've seen it.**

**You've sharpened your pencil on the cost and schedule: They know it.**

*The Client Interview has to be ALL ABOUT THE CLIENT.*

Members of competing teams may sound smooth and wear top-drawer threads. They will be charming, intelligent, and well-informed. But, today it takes more than smooth delivery.

In fact, **you might not sound all that "smooth," but, you can still win** because...

# *Today's client is sophisticated and especially wary of the old dog-and-pony "pitch."*

Winners see smiles among the people on the selection committee and looks of relief. Why? Do they channel Harry Potter™ and his magic wand?

No. But they *have* overcome something rampant in our business.

*They know they can't understand a client simply by browsing the Internet. They know they have to get up and out of their chairs before the interview...and prepare.*

# *Winners demonstrate an uncanny knowledge of the*

*client's project.*

*Winners seem to have a sixth sense for what the client actually needs.*

*Winners know how to solve the challenges of the project.*

**Let's look more at what clients really want and are really looking for during that interview.**

This is an accumulation of research I have done and countless other research efforts conducted, and the results are in...

# Fine Point #1
# You

We've established that clients are looking for key people at different levels of the project. If you're part of the boots-on-the-ground, day-to-day management of the project, they're looking primarily for you. After all, you are the one building their project, aren't you?

So, you're in the interview room. It's your turn to step up. Here's what's on their mind:

- **Do I like this person?**
- **Is she credible?**
- **Can they do the job?**
- **Can I trust him?**

You can relax. Now that you know they're **not** looking for a grinning game show host, just be your straight-forward, trustworthy self and convey ideas about their wants and needs.

Believe it: A marketing/research power-house **RainToday**™ surveyed 5,000 buyers in our industry, people in architectural and construction services, and the study showed that buyers simply want to know that the seller understands…that you understand their needs and situation.

# Fine Point #2
# Understanding

You will convey your understanding of the client's wants and needs when you show them you know the answer to these questions:

- **Why is this client building what they're building?**
- **Why are they renovating instead of building new or vice-versa?**
- **What is driving this project?**
- **Why do they need this project?**
- **What are they going to do with it?**

These are the kinds of questions you should have answered well in advance of the interview.

# Fine Point #3
# Present Appropriate Solutions

I really must stress this one:

**Your plan must fit their schedule.**
**It must fit within their budget.**
**Your solutions must fit the client's purpose and tolerance for risk.**

*Far-fetched ideas, without applicable client purpose, kill deals -* even when the client is a city council developing a high design art museum.

*The client needs to see working solutions* in your plan for visitor engagement, storage and delivery, various galleries, viewing, and gathering spaces, and public ingress and egress in harmony with existing infrastructure.

Without looking into the other parts of the client and how they operate, let's do this one more time. You must understand:

- **the client's business**
- **the client's needs**
- **the client's situation**

*...And how to make the client connect with your team.*

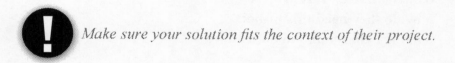 *Make sure your solution fits the context of their project.*

And always ask yourself...

## SO WHAT?

This is huge and a major hurdle for some teams. This is where our entire industry often falls down.

**We tend to fail when it comes to communicating the VALUE of our service.**

**We're all really good at telling WHAT we do and how we do it.**

**But we never say WHY we do what we do.**

**We seldom explain the value of our features and programs for the client.**

So, when I teach my workshops, I spend a lot of time asking, "So what? So What? So WHAT?"
"We do this – we do that...so what?"

Once you get used to communicating the value of your services from the client's point of view, you will make a much bigger connection with your client. Suddenly, they will understand the value, not just the features, you have to sell.

Lastly, we come back to that comfort level.

# Fine Point #4
# Create a Connection

***They Simply Felt "More Comfortable" With the Winning Team.***

Aauugggh! This one is so frustrating, isn't it? WHY did they feel more comfortable? HOW did this happen?

I've passed on the "client-more-comfortable" response to really good people who lost a final pitch. When they heard it, they just threw up their arms in frustration, rolled their eyes and howled, "What did I *DO?*"

Let's rephrase that question:

## What can you DO to create that comfort level?

We're talking about presentation **content**, of course, but we're also talking about **delivery and engagement**. We're talking about how we connect and make clients comfortable with us and our team.

I'm sure you've all heard the saying that in order for a customer to buy, they must **know**, **like**, and **trust** the company or sales person. That old saying holds true here as well. Your client must personally connect with you in order to buy.

The client must develop a sense of comfort with you and your team.

If you fail to make a connection, you fail to win the job.

Don't worry, we will talk more about how to create a stronger connection and comfort level with our audience, But first, we need to understand what differentiates our team and what stands out in our client's mind.

*No offense, but we all talk and sound a lot alike.*
*We all use the same means and methods.*

*How do we...*

DIFFERENTIATE?

## Behind the Scoreboard: How Clients
## Really Select Winning Teams

I recently worked with Teena Bergstrand, Senior Marketing Manager of one of Colorado's top construction companies, to develop an in-depth survey. The complete survey can be found on my website, *www.BeEvolutionary.com.*

We started with an online survey of around 120 people across 15 states. From there, I went out and personally interviewed 20 company owners, high level decision makers, who conduct interviews and select design and construction firms, as well as a few owners' reps who have similar responsibilities in the construction market.

A couple of points really jumped out of the survey and represented really deep problems. Here's one: **How does a team differentiate itself from others?**

Let's face it; design and construction hasn't changed a whole lot when we get into the field and start moving dirt. New things enter the big picture, now and then, but for the most part we all sound the same…

I know this after working with many contractors but here's a shocker:

I couldn't believe it when owners came back and said,

## *"We really CAN tell the difference between the teams."*

**From the client's perspective, what differentiates one construction team from another?**
We talked about attitude, but let's look at a bit more of the same... only different:

# Differentiator #1
## Personality and Attitude

- The very first thing that stood out was personality and attitude.
- It has to do with the way you might come off when problems come up.
- It also has to do with the connective personality of your TEAM.

- **Are you collaborative problem solvers?**
- **Do you work as a team?**

When problems rear their ugly little heads, will they feel comfortable contacting someone on the team?

**Are all team members approachable, or just a few, or only one?**

Clients look for:

**Team players**
**Lack of egos**
**Problem solvers**
**Team confidence**
**Good communicators**
**Approachable contacts**
**Nobody with a chip on their shoulder**

# *Beware of being overconfident. They will throw you out in an instant.*

- **They want confidence.**
- **They want problem-solving ability.**
- **They want personality and the right attitude.**

**They want a *TEAM PLAYER*.**

 *They want the person they can see themselves working with…over the duration of the project, in good times and in bad. One that is looking ahead and can solve problems when they arise.*

### Differentiator #2
### Team Culture

- How does your team handle adversity?
- How does your team celebrate success?
- How well does your team work together?
- How does your team interact as a team?

This is your team "culture."

**Team culture is critical, especially if you do a lot of design-build work: There is no "I" in team.**

So how do you convey a solid positive team culture during the interview? **Body language and communication.**

*Watch your body language in that interview! Clients pick up on non-verbal cues among team members. If sitting, have good posture. Lean slightly forward, attentive to your other team members' presentation. Nodding in agreement, showing support, respect, and acceptance.*

Do you like one another? HINT: Act like it!
Do you respect one another?
Have you worked together on other projects?

**Clients ask themselves:**

**"Are they going to have internal battles and in-fighting with one another?
Or, are they going to be a real team?"**

They will look at how you interface as a team.

Do you work as competing factions within the team?

Or do you work together?

***How you act is just as important...when you are NOT the speaker.***

How do you act when another team member is presenting? Are you sitting there **smiling**? Are you **scowling** or **rolling your eyes** as if to say, *"We don't do that. I can't believe he said that!"*

**This is critical. This is hard evidence of your team culture.**

If you sit back in your chair, if you look **bored** or even **grouchy**, if you **slouch** in your chair, if you **cross your arms** and look disengaged - or if you sit there with a mild **smirk** on your face –

...Here's what **the client thinks:**

"Look at these people. They don't even agree with each other. How are they going to work together on my building?"

 *When you're listening – smile, nod, or somehow indicate approval of what your team member has to say. You want that connection with your team, and the client, throughout the entire presentation.*

Your Team Culture is critical.

**That's one, very good reason *why* we get in a room and *PRACTICE*!**

**This is why we *practice several times* before that interview.**

**We practice to learn to *be together* and *respect each other*.**

This is critical with joint ventures and design build teams, given that the owner is even more aware of the dynamics between companies. Who is really in charge, who is calling the shots, can they work together? The dynamics go on and on....

That's what your client will be looking for.

# Differentiator #3
# Project Approach

When it comes to your technical experience and project approach, how are you going to design or build their project?

- **How are the challenges and risks presented?**
- **What solutions do you have?**
- **How can you help them?**

Even though it seems like we all deal with a project in similar ways, clients say we approach projects in slightly *different* ways. This is where our perceived differences begin.

Even your project phasing and your logistical plan, may be approached in different ways.

- **Do you go up?**
- **Do you go out from the center of the building?**
- **How do you run your electrical – do you go down, do you go up, do you go from the center out?**

All these things show how you phase that building during construction. All indicate the approach you are going to take when getting that building built.

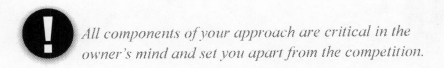

*All components of your approach are critical in the owner's mind and set you apart from the competition.*

They really want to know how you are going to design their project. Do you listen to them and understand their needs? Do you want their input?

And, they really want to know how you are planning to build that project, especially **from the superintendent's perspective**. That approach comes across differently among teams.

This is a great place for superintendents to really get engaged and talk in the interview. This is what they really love to do every day: Get their hands dirty and really figure out the job and the most efficient way to build the project.

Owners are interested in hearing how you plan to proceed and solve their issues.

## Differentiator #4
## Relevant-Similar Experience

Lastly, we get to that relevant, similar experience. This one's a little tricky these days.
Of course, you'll want to show what you've done in the past (shades of the dog-and-pony).
But, again, the real key is **how these past projects relate to THIS project**.

Once again, it's not about you.

*It's about them. You must connect the dots on how your other projects are similar and relate to their issues.*

Remember: The bygone days of trotting out a half dozen projects – right out of the gate – are over. Save relevant projects for later, much later. When you are addressing a concern this client has, you show a past project that solved that very issue! It has a much greater impact on the client when it is shown at the right time! That's why we save "relevant-similar experience" for last.

**Now they want to see how you have:**

- **Identified issues they will face.**
- **How you have successfully solved similar issues in the past.**

They want you to connect the dots more *specifically* when you display that project experience in direct correlation to the issues they face.

- When you have an issue – for example, in a downtown area with nearby water features such as a river or lake – you might have a very high water table. Maybe nearby projects run into ground water issues.

- If you're talking about a project like that and the client knows he's facing a ground water issue, this is where you say, *"Hey, we know you have this issue. Here's how we're going to handle it,"* and you show them your ideas on how to mitigate the issues.

- Then add, *"By the way, two blocks over, we designed this building and it's been dry for the two years since it was built. We addressed this exact same issue: We designed in the appropriate drainage and it's working. We've never had a drop of water."*

Think about it, when the timing is right:

*...Now, your past experience suddenly has real VALUE and EMOTIONAL MEANING.*

*...Your past projects NOW carry a lot more weight in the client's mind.*

*...Never try to run through a hum-drum list of projects in the beginning.*

1.  Everyone should have a stable of stories about relevant past projects in their hip pocket.

2.  Whenever you talk about a challenge or an issue, think about where you've done it before.

That's when you tie in that relevant experience.

That's when you become relevant, in your client's eyes, when it comes to building their project.

*DEMONSTRATE project relevance to client concerns and your projects will hold more weight and you'll be seen as the expert.*

# *Timing, Timing... It's All Timing! Connect those dots at the right moment with past projects.*

**At the end of the day – in your client's mind – it's going to come down to these four things:**

- Personality and attitude
- Team culture
- Project approach
- Relevant and similar experience

# 6

## GETTING READY
## STRATEGIES AND PRACTICE

**The people who don't know how to prepare, people who think they can wing it need...**

**...to Get Real**

## Establish Emotional Connections

We introduced this concept before! This is critical. When you have only a few minutes to tip the tables, always assume the other side has what you have: specs, data, dollars, and schedule. Every firm will say they can do it "on-time" and "on-budget."

You just need to nail-down one thing in their minds: "You are the team they want to work with."

So, what's the purpose of the presentation? This might be something of a paradigm shift for some of you, but it's critical to understand your purpose before you go in. We've already touched on the fundamentals:

- **Entertain**
- **Educate**

- **Inform**
- **Persuade**

Remember your first, fundamental priority:

**"When you go in...**
**...you want to win,**
**...so you must PERSUADE!**

Again, from a competitive standpoint, we know we can all "build the building." Now what?

**What can you do to make a difference?**

**How do you tip the scales in your favor?**

**How do you persuade the client you are the right choice?**

**How do you win the interview?**

## "Get Real" Phase 1
## PRACTICE!!

Owners want to know you've invested your time to learn about them and their project. They always seem to know if you haven't these days – like I said, times have changed.

Here's another example: The marketing people have put together a killer proposal, great 3D graphics, and the whole works. Thousands of dollars have been spent to deliver a top notch proposal. There's just one hitch:

*...the project manager who says he's "Got it...Down."*

This is what kind of frosts me, now and then. I've watch teams practically chant by the water cooler: "We've got to practice, practice…practice!" They do, too, most of them.

But maybe the project manager in this scenario thinks he's "got it down." Maybe he's done it a bazillion times. Why practice? He'd rather go to happy hour and watch the game (who wouldn't?).

Here's the Number One *fundamental* reason for this project manager's need to rehearse:

- **His competition spends a ton of time rehearsing.**

- **Competing teams spend 12 to 20 hours, *per person*, rehearsing.**

- **The "practice" element wins the big games. It wins Interviews, too.**

- **The Short List Client Interview is your BIG GAME.**

# *A fundamental paradigm shift has changed our industry over the last 20 years…*

# *…the amount of PREP time needed for the short-list interview.*

### Be the Drag-*er* not the Drag-*ee*

If you feel your team is dragging you into these meetings, chanting "practice" – and there *are* three or four practice sessions necessary – you now know why:

*Clients are more sophisticated.*
*Competitors have raised the bar.*
*Clients sense it when a project team isn't prepared.*

### "Get Real" Phase 2
### Save the Boilerplate for the Contract

#### *How to Give Your Client the Sizzle and the Steak*

For decades, presentations began with the presenting company braying in a tedious monotone about their "history of integrity and dedication to customer service," and, we might add, "Blah-blah in concert with blah-BLAH-BLAH blah-blah."

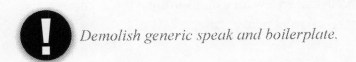

*Demolish generic speak and boilerplate.*

# *Project owners are uncannily smart. They sniff out "Blah-Blah Boilerplate" in a second.*

## *Insta-Cure for the "Blah-Blahs"*

- **People *love* to talk about themselves.**
- **They love to *hear* people talk about them.**
- **Encourage them to *talk* about themselves, whenever possible, before-hand.**
- **Reflect that feedback back to them *in the interview.***

Clients are proud of where they've been and what they do. Let them go into pre-interview conversations about who they are, how they wound up on the client committee – anything to reveal tidbits about their project concerns and what makes them tick.

In the interview, engage them. Ask them to start by telling you who they are, their role during the design and construction of the project and any concerns they have or any new developments and thoughts since the RFP came out.

If this sounds like casual conversation, it is, to a point. But chatting about a final, short list interview for a multi-million dollar competition is not. This is NOT a casual conversation.

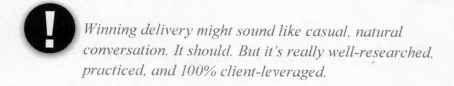

*Winning delivery might sound like casual, natural conversation. It should. But it's really well-researched, practiced, and 100% client-leveraged.*

Based on years of client surveys, you should know that clients:

- Spot "canned" boilerplate in seconds.
- Look for "canned" presentations to weed-out and disqualify.
- Dislike generic rhetoric. Anyone can be generic.

*Do Unto Others...*

The same **applies to everyone on the team**: If you get up there and give a canned talk about your quality control program...or your safety program...or your boilerplate logistics monologue...you can expect...what you...yourself...would do...are you...getting sleepy?

This can be very relaxing, but the client is in the process of being *hypnotized*! Not good!

That's right: **They actually nod off with their eyes open.** And, when it happens, an unwelcome "transformation" begins:

# *Keep the client ENGAGED – Talk about the SPECIFICS of their project.*

### How to Dis-engage (not good)

If, say, your Quality Control Program presentation fails to **immediately** tie-in to that client, if it fails to immediately make that instant connection with their project, you will sound canned.

Sounding canned and too generic means getting canned - on the spot - before you can turn a blade of dirt on their site.

## "Get Real" Phase 3
## Create a Conversational Tone

Who needs textbooks? Who needs rote memorization? Are we acting in a Shakespeare play? No! We are just talking with the client about their project and how we solve their concerns. This is the foundation to building and giving the best presentation we can in a very short time. It all begins with the right kind of preparation.

 *Well-prepped teams are conversational, play off of one another, and are interesting to listen to.*

Let's forget about:

- **Trying to memorize what you can't memorize.**
- **Struggling to be somebody you aren't.**
- **Trying to sell them.**

It's not about selling.
It's about knowing what they need and how you can help them...

 *BE the Presentation, STOP MEMORIZING, know what they want, and have a conversation about it.*

# *Tell them HOW you will solve THEIR concerns.*
# *That's what they want to know...*
# *You must go beyond what they already know*
# *...from the RFP!*

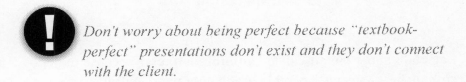

*Don't worry about being perfect because "textbook-perfect" presentations don't exist and they don't connect with the client.*

**You must Be *Yourself* when you present.**

**You must Be *Conversational*, professionally, which takes *practice*.**

**You must understand the vital need for *practice with your team*.**

**You must have professional *confidence* because nobody can say it like you can.**

**You must be prepared to make a great first impression.**

**SHOWTIME!**
**STAND AND DELIVER**

## Instinctive Strategies – Making the Right First Impression

Let's talk about our so-called **"animal instincts"** because they can sink us faster than a crocodile grabbing a water buffalo. You don't want to die because of something you did unconsciously, without even saying a word.

When you first walk into the room, **first impressions** are important, right? When you first go in and meet someone, you immediately create an impression of them in your own mind, don't you?

**Are they trustworthy?**
**Are they confident?**
**Can they do the job?**
**Do we like them?**
**Are they approachable?**

### 12 Impressions, 3 Seconds!!

There are roughly 12 decisions someone will make about you within three seconds after your first meeting. The process starts right then and the way you handle yourself is important. When you go in:

**Do you look approachable?**
**Do you have a smile on your face?**
**Do you look grumpy?**

Are you asking yourself...

*"Why did they bring me here?"*
*"Why am I in this interview?"*

Or are you walking in with...

**A good posture?**
**Your head held up?**
**Your eyes open wide?**
**A little smile on your face?**

**Do you have a friendly, approachable look that says you want to be there?**

Another way to improve the impression you make is by knowing the facility.

### Location Scouting

Check out the presentation room beforehand, if possible. This can be vital.

After doing a post-presentation de-brief with one of our clients, he said, "It was amazing to watch. I didn't even know we had a screen that lowered from the ceiling! Your team knew more about our conference room than I did."

1. The presenter had come in early, knew that he could push a button and that a projection screen came down from the ceiling. They went right to work, quickly setting up.

2. The client had been unaware they even had a drop-down projection screen in their own office! She said, "I didn't know we had a screen!" She looked at the others: "Did you know we had a screen?"

3. The team had accessed the building beforehand. They knew every little nuance about that conference room before their presentation began and it really impressed that selection committee.

What would have happened if they had been forced to ask for help? It could have been a real mess. The presentation would have been seriously delayed and the client would have become restless and irritable.

Anything you can do to improve that first impression can pay off in a big way.

 *Know in advance where the outlets are located and have your laptop booted up and ready to roll out your presentation...it's all crucial.*

*A smooth presentation set-up subliminally reflects your ability to work as a team. It subconsciously demonstrates your future efficiency on the job.*

*It can even reflect the perceived value of your brand.*

## Laptop At-the-Ready!

How many times have you seen someone sweating over how to start-up their own projector, **_fumbling through on-screen file folders_**, dashing to a briefcase, or scrambling for a connection cable? Annoying to watch, isn't it?

In this case, the presenter would have botched the pitch before opening his mouth.

Even worse, he now has to do an overwhelmingly good, over-the-top presentation, just to compensate for irritating the owner from the get-go. Know what happens? He over-compensates, looking desperate, irritable, and giving out any number of negative emotional cues.

You've heard people say, **_"The devil's in the details."_** Well, the little things add up. Those "little things" can make or break your proposal in the end.

Make it smooth and easy during set-up and the client is already comfortable with you and your team. That's how important it is to be prepared.

 _Nobody should ever look disorganized, confused and whispering, "Who's got the computer? Where's the port? Who's got the hook-up cable?"_

You will lose that interview before you even start.

## Get It Down

Watching someone fumble can be very annoying. People might empathize with your problem, but, they are also irritated because you look painfully inept.

Never stumble into the room in disarray, tripping over things, dropping things, fumbling with cables, looking confused about where computer connections should go or hissing things at each other, like: "Who's got the board, where's this, where's that?"

- **Make sure you have your logistics down when you walk in.**

- **Don't let one person carry too much.**

- **Rehearse how you will enter the room and how you will set-up.** Be aware of how you personally handle yourself during set-up.

- **A smooth set-up process is subliminally vital.** The owner needs to be thinking, "Wow, these people really have it together." It makes a difference.

These are *make-or-break* **first impressions!**

 *Everyone walking into that room should have practiced their role. They must know exactly where to go. They must know where to place equipment. They must know exactly how to set-up.*

## Strategic Furnishings

Sometimes you have enough room to create a U-shaped setting of tables. Clients would sit at the closed end of the table with your team on either side of the table near the opening. This is ideal.

- This way, everyone can see you, the screen, and the board.

- This way, when they are looking at the screen, they're always looking at you *and* the screen: That's what counts.

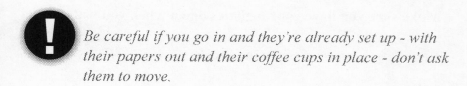

*Be careful if you go in and they're already set up - with their papers out and their coffee cups in place - don't ask them to move.*

That's uncomfortable enough to turn them off.

**Position your project manager, superintendent, or key personnel where they have the greatest eye contact with the client.**

- If you are in a situation with a long, boardroom table, always set your key people in the middle, directly across from the Client. So, whether watching the screen at the end of the table or each other, their eyes always go back to those focal points.

- As for project executives: The less day-to-day involvement they have with the job, the more off-center they should sit. I move them out of the way because I don't want the client looking at them all the time.

- Again, I want the client looking at the key people who are going to have the most day-to-day responsibility.

## Strategic Positions...for Eye Contact!

Let's talk more about eye contact. Rule Number One is EYE CONTACT. The greatest way to make connection and build trust with someone is that simple. I'll say it again: "**Eye Contact Rules.**"

Look at where you will be sitting in relation to where your client is sitting.

**Discover where you need to sit in order to have the best possible eye contact with the owner.**

You often have a long table in a conference room with **the screen at one end**; if the owner is on one side and you are sitting on the other side, this is fine until you start your slide show.

**Once the slide deck begins**, suddenly, everyone looks up at the screen, not across the table at each other.

**GET UP! Never just sit at the table if you are not in the right spot to have eye contact.**

Walk up to the screen, look back at the owner and look at the other people in the room. If you are the one speaking, you must get up so they can see you AND your visual, all at once.

Without that critical eye contact - when you are looking up at the screen instead of directly at me - I've just lost my connection with you.

 *Position yourself so you always have a direct line of sight with the client.*

Check out the "Be Trustworthy" section in Chapter Twelve for more tips on eye contact.

## *"<u>Un</u>-Polish" your Delivery...*

Here's one great thing about clients and interviews:

## **Clients are NOT looking for polished professional presenters or speakers.**

In fact, smarmy, overly polished speakers and presenters can raise suspicions and concerns. I know of companies that get dinged because they go into interviews overly polished.

Owners want to see a superintendent in jeans and work boots.

Owners want to see architects and engineers look professional, but not uptown New York City, unless that is where you're interviewing.

They want to see the team as smart, experienced, professional human beings.

This is a great thing to know:

*They don't look for perfection...they want connection. Remember back to the comfort and connection we spoke about earlier.*

Don't focus on the window dressing, just ask yourself:

- **How do I connect with the audience?**
- **How do I build that trust?**
- **How do I establish that credibility?**
- **How do I make them feel like they know me?**

How do you accomplish that?

**Be in the client's situation.**
**Be who you are.**
**Be the one they feel they can trust.**

**That's what they want. And**
**"that's when they buy".**

# *BE Who You Are.*

**!** *Execs - Be the "Suits." Supers - Wear the "Boots."*
*BE Yourselves.*

Since we are talking about dress, the rule-of-thumb here is to be dressed a level above your audience to show respect and dressed in accordance with your position on the project.

You don't want to overdress – you'd never wear a tie when presenting in a mountain ski resort community such as Vail, Colorado. And, you don't want to underdress – wearing a T-shirt to interview, even if it is a Saturday and the project is in a small town. Yes, these are both real stories that happened and didn't end well.

And when I say it is ok to wear boots and jeans – I mean clean work boots, near new, nice jeans or cotton-type slacks, and a tucked-in, button-down shirt that has been to the cleaners and is nicely pressed.

Get the picture? Professional, neat, crisp, clean – that is the look you are going for, not a look that says you just came from a job site.

### Things That Need Polish

It's easy for most people to pick out distractions and what a speaker is doing wrong. I'm sure you've all noticed these before and are aware of what not to do, but I'd be remiss if I didn't mention them in a presentation handbook. Just as important as not being overly polished, you don't want distractions that take away from your message.

We talked earlier about creating a comfort level and connection with our audience. And, our audience isn't looking for perfection; however, if the speaker has an annoying habit that is creating a distraction, the listener will eventually begin to focus on that and stop listening, thus, destroying any comfort level that was being formed.

1. **Stay still.** This means planting your feet… no dancing, swaying or pacing. Pretend you are an old oak tree, firmly rooted into the ground. Your base – the trunk – doesn't move. Not even in the strongest winds.

2. **Move with purpose.** When you want to move, do so and do it with purpose. This creates meaningful movement and stops the distraction of swaying and pacing. Moving without purpose is distracting and makes the speaker look nervous.

3. **Use your hands.** Most people get into trouble when they try to keep their hands down. Inevitably they end up getting clasped behind the back or in front in what I call the fig leaf position or holding on to one another in a death grip or twisting motion. Keep your hands up and apart and use them in appropriate gestures that reinforce your message.

4. **Be heard.** If they can't hear you, they can't trust you. Your volume when you are the presenter should be 20% louder than your everyday voice. You want your voice to carry the room and be easily heard. Remember to use pauses and emphasis words, and give some variances to your speech. You don't want to be monotone and put your listener to sleep! In other words, BE Passionate – Chapter Twelve has more on this!

If you have more questions about how you look or sound, simply video yourself. You will immediately see and hear what is distracting and what things you want to correct.

Now you are ready to stand and deliver your message with ease and confidence.

# 8

## BREAKING IT DOWN
## STRONG OPENING HOOKS

### *How to "Blow-It" Sky High*
### ...in 8 Seconds!

Back to the old-fashioned dog-and-pony show: This is where stodgy old XYZ Company files into the room. The firm's principal opens, as always.

On cue, he says something canned in an **excruciatingly boring monotone**, something like...

*"Thank you. We are very excited to be here. We have put together the A-Team and we are the best for your project..."*

...Something like that. Then, they meander through the firm's history. Then, they've got to show some projects. I mean, they invested all kinds of money in all that slick photography – they've got to show that off, right?

For you, this is great. They're playing right into your hands: Poor old XYZ is lost in tradition and mucking through their old-fashioned slide shows.

The client doesn't want the old-fashioned dog-and-pony show. They want to know more about themselves. If the XYZ principals bray on-and-on about *themselves,* they'll perish with all the other dinosaurs.

Get off *the topic of* you *and immediately* start talking about them!

### Eight Seconds to Ground Zero

The average audience attention span is just eight seconds - shorter than a sneezing fit. People have "zero" patience these days.

# *In our tweeting, email, video-streaming society, studies show that you can lose your audience in EIGHT seconds!*

**Repeat: I said, "EIGHT SECONDS" and counting!**

**While you're in that room, you need to keep your audience engaged for 20 to 30 minutes.**

Here's the problem: Even a well-practiced team won't get to the project approach until they're almost halfway through the pitch. That's the problem.

Poor old XYZ & Associates. They've given their windy introductions. They're gone relentlessly on about their excellent team. Now, oh-no, there they go, drifting off about their company history…and…their… experience…and…

**They just keep putting the client more…and…more…*AND more*…to…sleep.**

When it's our turn, how do we keep the client engaged?

- How do we keep the presentation focused on THEM?
- How do we keep their interest level up?
- How do we keep them from "booing" us out of the room, in their minds?

**When it's our turn, how do we keep them from falling asleep with their eyes open?**

# Oh, and…

# ...About those old-fashioned slide shows:

# They're dead.

### Being Interesting...Preliminaries

Being interesting. Hmm. We have eight seconds. No slide show. How?

**Focus on the client and their needs when you prep your interview:** What do you know about what they know, about their background, their experience, their concerns, and what their hot buttons might be?

How technically design and construction savvy are they? That's a big one.

If you start throwing out industry acronyms, are they going to understand them? Do they need more "show and illustrate," more demonstrations and examples? If they are not an industry-educated group, you need to know in advance.

Or, once again, you will lose your audience.

## Winning Presentations and Flow

So, what is the winning presentation agenda going to look like? How do we make that connection? And, hold the interest of the audience?

### Opening Hook

We want to open with a Hook. That opening hook should be the following, right out of the gate:

"What can you do for that client?" What is your promise? What are you going to deliver? Make a bold statement upfront that makes them sit up and listen and shows you understand their needs.

### Opening Introductions

Here, we talk about team introductions and how every team member can connect with someone on that selection committee. It's not just who you are, your name, and your years of experience – No! Your introduction is not a recap of your resume; it's all about the value that you bring to that client. (In the next Chapter, I'll walk you through a formula for stronger introductions.)

### Approach/Keys to Success

You need to identify three main topics – three keys to success – showing what you bring to the table…what you can do for them. And that you understand the issues surrounding their project.

This is where you bring in your project experience. Show them where and how you've done it before.

## *Project experience: That's what they want to hear…but, only when the timing's right… and*

*now's the time. After you discuss their needs and challenges, you show PROOF where you have solved similar issues before: This is your project experience.*

### Summarize Value

Bring it all together with brief, strong value-points as to why they should select your team.

Let's discuss each one of these parts in more detail.

### STRONG STARTS
### How to Deliver Your "Opening Hook"

Here's where we pull away from the pack.

*Roughly 99% of the companies out there start with some version of the following, canned, boring, speech - sure to put your client to sleep more quickly than a master hypnotist:*

I call it the "I-Speech."

### The Erroneous "I-Focused" Opening

*"Thank you for allowing us to present to you. We are excited to be here today. I am the president of ABC Construction and I would like to introduce you to our team that we have put together for this project.*

**Excited? No, they aren't. No way.**

Maybe we gravitate to this one because our mothers taught us to have manners and be polite. But, how polite is it, really, when you know your audience has an attention span of EIGHT SECONDS?

The presenters in this scenario have already lost their audience. They are showing them they are just like everyone else and they're already putting them to sleep…and what have they said?
**Nothing.**

**Don't let your team members do this. Make sure they don't waste those valuable eight seconds.**

The presenters above started talking about themselves. As the client, "I" want them to start out with things related to ME.
How are you going to help me?
What do you know about me?
How do you eliminate or minimize my risk?

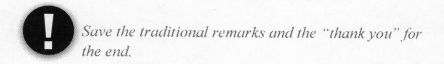

*Save the traditional remarks and the "thank you" for the end.*

## A NEW Beginning

You need your own originality and style – of course – but, looking right at the client, here's a good way to start:

*"You are losing potential revenue because you don't have enough student housing. I am (**Your Name**), and over the next 30 minutes, we are going to show you how we will deliver your new student*

*housing...a Full Semester Early...and help you generate $1.2 million in additional revenue."*

Do you see the difference? Wow. Note the pause before and another after "...a full semester early..." Don't forget to pause for impact when it really counts.

**This is why you are here. Start with impact. Immediately show them how you will bring the owner the solution she needs.**

From the very first words out of your mouth, let them know...

- WE KNOW you're losing potential revenue.
- WE KNOW you don't have enough housing on campus.
- WE ARE HERE with your solution.
- WE WILL DELIVER your solution AHEAD OF SCHEDULE.
- WE ARE going to SAVE YOU MONEY.

**This is the ONLY way to begin the first eight seconds of your presentation.**

How do you think the owner will react to THAT in eight seconds? They are going to sit up and listen, right? Depending on the people on the client committee, they might even have made the decision to hire you, right then.

**From there, they are probably thinking, "Really? Tell me how? Can you really do this?"**

In other words, all you have to do is deliver the rest of your presentation without blowing the impression you just made.

From this point forward...

- **Back up what you just said with brief, to-the-point illustrations.**

- **Demonstrate how you will bring about this solution.**
- **Build trust by showing them you've done it before.**
- **Have a dynamic Q & A session.**
- **Thank them for their time.**
- **Pack up and leave as efficiently as when you walked in.**
- **You just won yourself a project.**


## Proof Positive

I know this works because we actually used this presentation not long ago.

We won the job.

At the end of the interview, the client did say:

*"Okay, you made a really bold promise, here. If you can show us you can do it, you've got the job."*

The client invited our team to return the next day, this time with our entire technical staff - the same people who worked on the schedule and the estimate.

They had to walk the client through the full-blown schedule to illustrate how things were going to be done. They had to prove what we'd said the day before. Of course. But we were IN!

# *Never say something you can't deliver. Just deliver the end-results, first.*

Do it with to-the-point brevity.

**That's "The Tell."**

**"The Show" - the proof - comes later.**

### "Proof" Proven

Another part of the proof came in the form of being able to show a similar project, one we had completed on a similar scale, with a similar budget and delivery deadline. That always helps to shore up your proof.

In this case, we had previously put up a student housing project on a nearby campus for another university. It was almost the exact same project and with the same architect. So, we gave the client solid proof in a visual context that said, "Hey, we can do this."

We got the job.

---

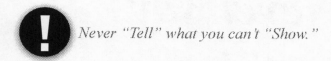
*Never "Tell" what you can't "Show."*

### "No Lie…"

Your opening statements must have a solid foundation in fact. Always work from your own work-ups, drawings, estimates, all of it. Take it all down to the bare essentials of what you can offer the client…*in eight seconds flat.*

- **Make sure you and everyone on your team feels confident about what you can deliver.**

- **If you have a non-believer on your team, the client will see it in a heartbeat.**

- **Work out before hand any doubts among any of your team members.**

- **NEVER LIE and tell the client you can do something that you can't.**

*This is what practice is all about. Yes, it takes time, but it is well worth it when you have discovered that winning hook – the solution to their problem.*

All doubts and potential dissension come up in practice sessions and sometimes solutions may not surface immediately. This is why we have several meetings.

After people have had time to dwell on the project – as related to the upcoming presentation – is when questions, concerns, and solutions come up. That's another key reason why you need more than just one or two practice sessions.

*When you walk in with your Eight-Second Intro...*

*Make sure every single person on your team is 100% comfortable and confident about*

*...everything*

*...on the table.*

*Clients remember the warm feeling they get from a team's unified sense of confidence. They will feel more comfortable with your team.*

When you have it, you're ready.

### Hit 'Em Now!
When you and your team have that confidence, when everyone knows what you can bring to that client, Don't Save It for Later!

***Hit 'em with it right at the top***...right from the get-go.

If you do, they are going to sit up and be engaged for the next 30 minutes instead of sitting there the whole time half-asleep in their chairs.

***From the start, you want them to sit up and think, "Tell me more about how you can do that for me."***

## The Owner-Focused Opening

Here's another Sample Scenario:

***"We know your budget is tight for the renovation of your*** (insert **name of their project)** ***and we know you're interested in our perspective of your budget. We have good news for you today. I am*** (insert name), ***President of ABC Construction and here is the team that will make that budget work."***

- Here, again, in about eight seconds, you just differentiated yourself from your competitors; you have the client sitting up and paying attention.

- You have them anticipating your every word because, now, you're hitting the heart of their biggest concern.

- You have said, beginning with that first sentence: *"We know your budget is tight for the renovation of your (project)."*

First, we're naming *their* project, *specifically.* We're using specifics about *them.* If you know about their project, their budget, correct: and their schedule, you have to use those specifics.

*We can't just use clichés, talking about being "on-time, on budget." Everybody does that. ...Everybody but the people on your team, because you are not going to sound like everyone else.*

Remember: Within those crucial eight seconds, people form lasting opinions about *you.* Believe me, it gets personal, too.

*If you start out flat, clichéd, boring, and spouting boilerplate, they subconsciously already want you to lose.*

- Name the project
- Use specifics
- Hit their major concerns immediately

That's what an Opening Hook is all about.
You must have an Opening Hook to connect.
You have eight seconds to make that connection.

 *Don't speak in generalities... "your project" "on-time and on-budget"... Use specifics. State the name of the project, use the opening date and what their budget is!*

This is how you start your overall presentation. This is how you start all your individual sections.

*Anytime you change speakers, whenever it's time to get up and deliver your part, your Opening Hook still applies. Let's look further at section openers...*

## Game-Changing Section Openers

- Every section of your presentation needs a hook to establish that connection with the client.

- Every section presenter has eight seconds or less to create that need to hear more on the part of your audience.

- I'm not saying that you should use them, verbatim. Just use them as guidelines to craft your own opener with the right hooks for your client.

That said, know that these Section Openers have actually been successfully used to get winning results:

### Sample Section Opener #1
*You could say...*

"Your project is surrounded by neighborhoods. We understand your desire to minimize disruptions. Our 'Good Neighbor Program' will do just that."

In this situation, presenters make the immediate connection – showing they understand one of the owner's concerns and how they are going to mitigate that.

## *Sample Section Opener #2*

The same thing goes for safety issues, which are almost always a concern for most clients, especially clients dealing with schools. Don't open up saying, "Now, let's talk about safety..." You need to make a connection and talk about safety and how it pertains to your client specifically.

This one delivered the message with impact:

*"Safety is paramount! This is an active campus with 30,000 students and faculty. Here's how we minimize disruptions and keep them safe."*

This is where we launch into our safety program and how we're going to keep everyone safe. See the difference here?

The client is going to sit up immediately, take notice, and listen to the rest of what you have to say. When looking at your content and formulating the crux of your presentation, first think: "What do I want them to remember?" Then think brevity:

- **This will reinforce what you have to say.**
- **It will help you to be concise.**
- **It will minimize the number of words you need.**

The overall effect will have a *greater impact on your audience*. The goal, here, is to allow your audience to really, truly hear the benefits of what you have to say.

- **They will remember what you said.**
- **They will remember your team.**

Your team will NOT be associated with some mind-numbing, rambling blur of wordy clichés attached, in the back of their minds, to some of your competitors.

*When you sit down to outline your message, think of the few, not the many. Forget about the mundane processes. Focus only on the strong points you want them to remember. Start with THAT.*

…And end with that. Try them out on your team. Again, this is why practice is critical. If you put your own team to sleep with a meandering list of irrelevant points, how will you connect with the owner?

*Remember: Your owner's attention level will be highest when you begin your talk.*

1. After you write down a key point, boil down that statement. Condense it down, again. I mean, really narrow it down.
2. Dwell on the impact of the meaning.
3. Do that and you will connect with the client. They will not only hear what you say, they will also remember how you made them feel; they will remember you and your team.

Look at this way: You can go on for five or ten minutes about safety. But what do they really need to know? They need to understand the following:

- **That safety is paramount.**
- **That safety is your top priority.**
- **That their staff/faculty/students must be safe.**
- **That you understand the importance of safety as much as they do.**

Here, you can also begin to see how we wrap the impact of your section into their overall project. Your piece of the presentation becomes a critical "take-away" part of the bigger picture.

*"We know you're concerned about it. We can fix it. We have a plan to deal with it."*

Pull in a key fact or figure. Make sure it makes sense for their vision of the project. Now, you're talking about them. See the difference? Start with a short, strong, impactful statement. Then, back it up with brief, strong essential points.

*Make your message come alive by seeding the old boilerplate with new information – THEIR information. Weave in the specifics about their project.*

All of a sudden the client loves you because, "Presto!" It's ALL ABOUT THEM!

# INTRODUCTIONS THAT CONNECT AND TRANSITIONS TO MAINTAIN THE FLOW

## Introducing Your Team

We've covered the basics of strong openings. Next, we move on to introductions, not only the care and handling of them, but, where and when to give the introduction of your team for the most impact.

As always, we want to make the connection with our audience. Now we want them to connect with the relevance of our people. We now want to make our people become, in their minds, a critical group they cannot do without.

A long-winded rehash of their resume is not going to cut it.

### "Introductions That Connect"

This is where we develop essentials that, in a few words, establish your value (or not).

This is where the client should get the feeling, **"Wow, I've gotta' have this guy for my project!"**

Just step up with a friendly, approachable attitude – not necessarily an overbearing grin unless that works for you – and share the essentials of who you are and how you are going to help the client. The essentials include:

**Your Name**

**Your Role** in the project (not your title)

Ah, there's a glitch for most people: Your "role" is not your title. Titles are nebulous. Titles can mean anything or nothing.

# *Maybe you're...*

## *"The Principal in charge,"*
## *"The Project Executive,"*
## *"The King of Construction,"*
## *"The Emperor of Estimates,"*
## *"The Pharaoh of Finance"*

# *...WHO CARES?*

# *WHAT'S THAT to a CLIENT?*

# Focus on Your Role!!

- **What is your day-to-day function on this project?**

- **What are you doing for them?**

- **What issues do you solve?**

- **Do you work with tight budgets?**

- **Do you get schools open on time?**

- **Do you keep them safe?**

Whatever it may be, you want to connect with an issue that will resonate with that client.

# Focus on Your Benefit!!

- **What will you deliver?**

- **What will you be able to achieve for them?**

- **What will you bring to the project?**

# Focus on Your Proof!!

This takes practice. Pare it down to your best essentials.

- **Where have you done it before?**

- **What in your resume builds credibility for THIS project?**

## *"One or two will do"*

The key elements of your introduction don't necessarily have to be in this order. But with these essentials in mind, starting with your name, avoid your lofty-sounding credentials and accomplishments (because your competitors have those, too) and **say something like this:**

*"I'm Bob, your Money Guy. We know your budget is extremely tight. It's my job to save money and I have a few ideas to share with you. I just finished a project where we were able to reduce the budget by 16%. I'm confident we will get your project budget where it needs to be."*

Here we bring a little fresh air into the room. We've dispensed with formal sounding titles and windy boilerplate. It takes us away from saying, "Good afternoon, I'm Bob, vice president of preconstruction and I've been with ABC Company for 30 years. I've done a hundred schools just like this...blah, blah-blah, blah-BLAH!" Go into all of the above and you really haven't shared much with the owner.

But, from "Bob, your Money Guy," the owner gets some tangible substance to grab and hold. He comes away with a better understanding of how you will save him money. He knows you want to work within his budget. That's what he's looking for. Who cares about your 30 years in the business and 100 projects building who-knows-what? That's all in the past.

*You want to focus on the present. What and how you can help them on this project.*

Here, Bob's a construction estimator who says he knows how tight the budget really is. He says things like:

*"I know your budget's extremely tight, but, I've never worked on a project that didn't have a tight budget. Well, I've got some good news for you today. We found ways we can save you money. On the last job I completed, we were able to cut 16% out of their budget and achieve XYZ."*

- **The client now knows Bob understands tight budgets.**

- **Bob will be there to protect his budget.**

- **Bob's a "tight budget" expert.**

- **Bob saved 16% on his last project.**

By now you can see how short these introductions need to be!

## SHORT introductions

A typical introduction should **never be more than 30 to 45** *seconds*. How many windy 10-minute introductions have we had to sit through in our long careers? You know where I'm coming from. Well, the client has been there, too, and no one wants to sit through that.

**Introductions need to be:**
**Short**
**Clean**

**Crisp**
**Memorable**

You can do this while giving out a lot of information you want the owner to hear.

**Here's another sample introduction:**

*"(Name), I'm your superintendent, your day-to-day leader in the field. I'll drive your schedule and make sure we complete your new school by August 1. In my 15 years as a superintendent, I've never finished a project late."*

WHAM! Nailed it, didn't he? You can tell them all the schools you've built later. But for starters, this is what they really NEED to hear.

What does the owner get from the superintendent? He gets a real sense of Confidence.

He's thinking, *"Yeah! This guy can DO it!"* because we all know that school projects live and die by the schedule. If we can't open before the start of school, in time for teachers to get in there and prep for their fall classes, everything falls apart. This is not good.

See the difference in the introductions above? The objective is to…

1. **Quickly make those connections.**
2. **Let them see the issues you can solve.**
3. **Give them one or two bits of evidence.**
4. **Cut through resume facts and figures to your project-specific credibility!**

**Again, I'm not trying to give you a list of things to memorize. Just a way to make a stronger connection.**

# *The best kept presentation secrets are not about memory.*

# *They are all about understanding.*

**!** *I want you to be able to get inside the owner's head, not to manipulate but to help them understand what you can do for them. And I want you to be able to accomplish that in a short amount of time.*

If you can do that and save someone from having to suffer through a boring, irrelevant presentation, they will love you for it.

Trust me. I've been there.

I'm a veteran of both sides of the presentation world - from the old days of traditional presentations to the winning formulas you've already discovered in this book.

Mainly, just get in there, deliver, and get out - without all the traditional ho-hum boilerplate.

Make it about the client. Make it stick. Make it count.

Let's wrap up this section with a quick note about transitions. How do you move from one speaker to the next?

Hint: It's not by saying "Thank you, Joe. Now, I want to tell you about...." NO! This is awkward and breaks the flow. You also don't want to use an equally bland statement like "Now, Joe will talk about the schedule...." SO WHAT?

Instead, do one of these two choices; First, the current speaker can simply summarize their part and stop, thus allowing the next person to put in a transition that paves the way for the next section.

"Now that you've heard how we control the cost and keep your project within your budget, let's look at how we are going to get your school open by August 1."

This transition ties right into your hook and sets the stage for the audience to WANT to listen.

Second method: The speaker finishing up can deliver the transition line that tees up the next topic. Then, the next speaker can go directly into their hook and strong opening.

*Good transitions are focused on the client, their needs, and their issues!*

# 10

## PAYING ATTENTION PICKING UP ON CLIENT CONCERNS

Owners see key issues in ways that differ from our perspective.

For example, how would you illustrate and talk about a project schedule?

Most of us want to talk about it in a very logical, detailed way that explains the flow and sequencing of events. We show how we can adjust for challenges as they arise, and keeps us on track or recover, if a set-back does occur.

…Not owners. For most, this is too much detail and doesn't connect with their true concerns. And, remember you only have 20 minutes for the entire presentation.

**I've seen contractors show up with eight-page (or more) schedules wanting to walk through it during an interview and they want to show it on the screen!**

*How are you going to talk about it in front of the client?*

**SO, they come back with a condensed, eight-*line* version**. Better. Not quite there…but, better.

Then, they involve their graphic designers, add color and highlight milestones with little stars.

**But, in the end, we still ask ourselves, "So what?" This was, still, all about us and how we schedule a project. The client's true concerns about the schedule issues had fallen off the wagon.**

We knew we had a problem from a presentation point of view. This type of old school schedule does not make a connection with the client. It does not show that you understand the client's needs and challenges.

- **How do you convey** what the client wants to hear in quick, meaningful brushstrokes?

- **How do you connect** with the owner's issues?

You need to do a full-blown schedule so you understand the project! And you can bring it to the interview; you just don't go over the full-blown, eight-page version during the interview. For the situation above, we show the owner benefits from the way we schedule, and at the same time show our methodology.

**You start by talking about their main concern – getting the project open for a big event, fast tracking the project in order to minimize disruptions, etc. Then, highlighting the critical items that must occur to hit that end date. It may be just another scheduling logistical challenge for you that is easy to overcome. For the client, it's often a source of high anxiety, often a "make-it-or-break-it" scenario.**

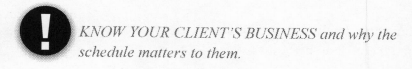

*KNOW YOUR CLIENT'S BUSINESS and why the schedule matters to them.*

# High Anxiety – High Risk

I want you to feel the client's anxiety. BE the client. What happens if the opening date is missed? What is at risk for them? Their clients? Their image? This is how you win presentations.

- The stadium is delayed? Where is the big game played? What happens to the 50,000 fans with tickets?

- School couldn't open on time. How would parents and teachers react?

- Schedule failure would leave new home owners / renters literally out in the cold.

- If the new hotel isn't open until January, you miss the holiday season.

*The owner is thinking not only about the welfare of his visitors, patients, etc., but, also about issues like major brand credibility.*

**All of the above put a lot of pressure on the client to select the designer or contractor who can perform! No excuses!**

## Solution: Go Straight to the Benefits!

Sensing the client's anxiety and understanding what is driving the schedule from the client's perspective, the contractor made a few changes on the schedule graph.

**They said,** *"By going with this schedule, we're able to deliver the project four months early - so you can take advantage of the holiday season. You can be open and taking reservations for Christmas and, most importantly, for New Year's Eve, which is always a big draw for downtown hotels like yours."*

**The owner loved it.**

He could glance at a simple visual chart and see his concerns were met.

Gone were the original eight pages of fine print.

**He immediately saw what he needed to see: An opening date that would make him money!**

Look at the routine information about the project that you want to share with the client... schedule, budget control, design process. How can you tailor it and make it more interesting? Something the client will relate to and connect with?

## *Your* Schedule...Is it "All" About *Them*?

You need to make it all about them. You need to make it easy for them to digest at a glance. Ask yourself the following questions:

- **Why did you schedule the project the way you did?**
- **What was your methodology?**
- **What issues or challenges does it eliminate?**
- **How does that interface and connect back to client issues?**

Let's look at a more detailed example:

### Sample Traffic Management Plan

This was for a site logistics and traffic management plan for an addition project to a school that involved the construction site wrapping around school grounds. Obviously, it was a very touchy issue and one that had severe consequences if anything were to go wrong.

The contractor eased the client's fears when he said:

*"We know disruptions and safety are your big concerns. We've given a lot of thought to our site logistics plan that will keep your students and faculty safe and minimize disruptions to the school day and the learning.*

*First, we'll get our crews on site early. Our crews will be settled and already working when surrounding residents leave for work and as faculty and students arrive, thus, not creating any extra traffic in the mornings.*

*Next, we will only allow deliveries to take place between 10:00 a.m. and 2:30 p.m. There will never be any additional traffic or deliveries impacting your site during drop off and pick up times.*

*That way, all of your students and staff will safely come and go.*

*Lastly, we will not allow any deliveries or 'loud' work – such as demolition or hammering the first week of May during testing days. We know the importance of maintaining a peaceful, quiet atmosphere for those days."*

So, how do you think the owner reacted when they heard all that? The owner knew:

- **We understood their daily schedule.**
- **We know their testing dates.**
- **We understand their campus.**
- **We understood their school.**
- **We will stay out of their way and not impact traffic.**
- **We care about them.**

*When you solve their most glaring concerns and show you care, the selection committee knows they want you for the job.*

**These issues seem routine to you, but some at the table have never been "here" before.**

As educators love to point out: An imagination can be a powerful thing. When educators visualize their school grounds in turmoil, that's unacceptable!

**It is your job to show them why "turmoil" is not going to be an option – not on your watch.**

So, as you cover the topics you feel you have to talk about in every interview, I challenge you to think about one thing, every step of the way:

**Are you talking about your issues...or theirs?**

How do you create that paradigm shift?

How do you make the switch - from you to *them* - so you can really connect on issues that keep them up at night?

The situations above are good examples of "Memorable Content."

## Memorable Content

1. Ask yourself, "What do you want your audience to remember?"
2. Which of their issues are most important and need to be addressed?

3. Less is more. Be concise, focus on what is most important for greater impact.
4. Streamline your message and reinforce it with every speaker.

Ask yourself the following questions:

- **Is it about the client?**
- **Are team members veering into generic boilerplate?**
- **Have they boiled down content to specifics?**
- **Are they staying out of the weeds?**

Make sure your team members quickly...

- Tie together key points.
- Show that client needs are understood.
- Show appropriate solutions.

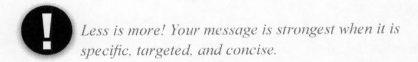

*Less is more! Your message is strongest when it is specific, targeted, and concise.*

Now, let's put it all together into a presentation concept you might want to memorize.
It's called ...

# "I-F-B-P"

**The IFBP Formula is simple, yet powerful, and should be committed to memory.**

Okay, I know I just broke my own memory rule, but this one's easy. I only wish I could remember where I first learned it.

I've used this formula, far and wide, when presenting training workshops for major firms of all kinds in our industry. I still use it today because it is simply the best, most solid formula I've ever heard of. It works.

**The "I" stands for "Issues" and "Interest."** (These two are interchangeable because client-related Issues always Interest the client.)

The "I" is all about the client. What are their issues and interests? What information do they need from you? This, also, immediately connects you to the client because you are talking about them.

**The "F" stands for the "Features."** What Features do you have to offer the client? This is the HOW you go about addressing and solving their issues.

- Scheduling benefits?
- Safety plans?
- Quality control strategies?
- Sub-contractor management techniques?

A feature highlights "How We Do It." Caution: Don't fall into the rut of regurgitating boring processes – keep it specific to their project – and don't let yourself fall into the weeds.

**The "B" stands for "Benefits."** What are the benefits of what we do? What will the client get by hiring you? Again, be specific – it is far more than your firm delivering a project on time and on budget!

And, finally,

**The "P" is for "Proof."** This is the proof we always have waiting in the wings, ready to back up the impact of the great presentation we just made.

This is our evidence, our past successes we've achieved. This is our stories of how we've helped other clients and this is what gives our prospective clients trust in us.

**Take a moment to commit it to memory: I-F-B-P**

**I**nterest/Issues
**F**eatures
**B**enefits
**P**roof

Write it down. Keep it handy.

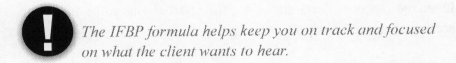

*The IFBP formula helps keep you on track and focused on what the client wants to hear.*

Use the IFBP Formula as an easy reference to connect with the client. Use the formula to show the value you have to offer.

Here's an example of a "Client Needs Matrix." You can put the IFBP formula to work if you draw a simple chart with the following:

# Sample Client Needs Matrix

| Client Need or Problem "The Issue" | What is our solution based on experience and ability? WHAT do you deliver? | What is the BENEFIT to the client based on my solution? | Example PROOF to back up this benefit |
|---|---|---|---|
| Build new dorms

House more students on campus | Get first wing open early | Generate $700,000 additional income

Save $60,000 in general conditions | Same team completed similar project on another campus |

Over the top of a horizontal line, the chart is separated into four sections from left to right:

- **Client Needs/Issues**
- **Our Solution – Experience/Value/Features**
- **Benefit to Client**
- **Example/Proof**

Addressing items listed along the line above, going left-to-right, we see four corresponding sections:

- **Building new dorms; housing more students**
- **First wing open early**
- **Generate $700,000 additional income; save $60,000 in costs**
- **Same team completed similar project on another campus**

You're already familiar with this situation, of course. Now you can see how it works in a graphic for the presentation screen or on a white board for training purposes with your team.

- Back to the opening hook: They need new dorms on their campus.
- Student housing is maxed out.
- They're actually losing freshman enrollment because they have nowhere to put their students.
- So, they need more dorms and they need them now.

**What is our solution going to be – what Features do we have to offer? In this scenario, we looked at the options and realized, *"Hey, we can get a wing done early."* That, alone, could win a project just like this one.**

- Now, the Benefit is the client can generate $700,000 in additional income from the rentals of those beds.

- And, they will save $60,000 in general conditions because we can complete the wing four months ahead of schedule.

- It's simple enough to dig up this kind of information. We went to the school web site and found the rates for a single bed in the existing dorms and did some simple math.

**Here, your Proof is critical.** We completed a similar project, with the same results, on a nearby campus! We were able to show the same, basic results, and built vital credibility and trust with our client.

# *The IFBP Matrix helps us mentally balance key elements*

# *during the prep phase of the presentation.*

IFBP elements are critical to your presentation:

1.  **They represent the key wants, needs, and challenges of the client.**
2.  **They are the "edge" in your team's presentation content.**
3.  **They differentiate you from the competition.**

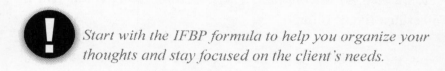

*Start with the IFBP formula to help you organize your thoughts and stay focused on the client's needs.*

You will run into variations. Sometimes you will have different versions of the strongest Proof. But, now you know where to begin in order to establish credibility with your client.

**Spoon-feed this information to them if you have to!**

**Hit them over the head, if need be!**

**Do whatever you need to do to show your benefits and how you will mitigate risks and solve their challenges better than your competitors.**

With all things said, done and behind you…

# *Now we're down to the last seconds...*

# *It's time to Stick Your Landing.*

# STICK THE LANDING
# FINISH AND CLOSE STRONG

## How to "Stick the Landing"

This is huge during international gymnastic competitions. We all know how they fly off the balance beam and try to "Stick the Landing":

- They must drop straight down.
- They must land on the mat without moving their feet.
- Then, the judges take over.
- This is the make-or-break factor in their final score.
- Trip or stumble and they're done.

Have you ever felt like this after making the final comments in an otherwise excellent presentation?

How do you wrap up and conclude the presentation?

Many firms want to give the "Why Us" slide or "Top 10 List." It sounds like a good idea, until you see another firm's list. Guess what? It's the same list – or very close…

Does this look familiar?

Why ABC Firm...
- Over 30 years experience in this market type
- Experts in student housing
- Experience on this campus
- Experience with team members
- Committed to safety
- Principal involvement on all projects
- 15 LEED® Gold Projects

SO WHAT? These are features of your firm and not unique to your firm. Remember, once you've made it to the short list, the client believes every firm is qualified to do the project. Don't leave them with a bland list that sounds like everyone else.

You need to persuade them you are the best firm for them.

Go back to the opening hook! Conclude by reinforcing what you can do for them – how you are going to reduce their risk and what makes you the right team to do so!

If we go back to our example, we might say something like this for our closing, "Over the last 30 minutes, we have shown you how we are the team that can get your student housing open a semester early, allowing you to keep your freshman enrollment strong. This solution will also save you $60,000 in general conditions and help you generate $700,000 of revenue.

Thank you for your time and consideration today; we look forward to working with you."

If you blow your summary and botch the closing, you risk losing the project.

# *Stick the Landing, summarizing your value. Give them the expected outcome and...*
# *Get Out!*

## 12

## PUTTING IT ALL TOGETHER "BE" THE WINNING PRESENTATION

I call them the **BEs** and they are vital qualities for any presenter.

I had a set of beverage coasters made with the winning BE qualities and tips, I hand them out in my workshops to remind participants of the key qualities that owners and clients look for during an interview.

**My workshop attendees can set their coffee mugs on them during practice sessions** or pin them to their office wall before an interview. Since we may never actually meet, I've included these tips in this book.

**Make printouts of the highlights below and post them in your practice room.**

**Think of these as Communicator Power Tools for the Winning Mind.**

In fact, they can be useful for all aspects of your life, from first introductions to re-connecting old friendships.

**They *really* come in handy in presentations and will help you BE THE WINNING PRESENTATION.**

**My Number One Rule!**

You can grin. You can dance. But if you use certain telltale words, the game's over before you begin.

You may not be aware of it but you probably use "**Wimpy Words**" when you talk to others.

These pesky, little telltale **indications of negativity** are an open window to your inner feelings about the client, your team, your company, you name it. These words...

Reveal your underlying **fear**.
They uncover your **uncertainty**.
They show your **lack of confidence.**
They equate to **lack of commitment** to the project.
AND they are not persuasive!

# From Glossary for Wimps

## "Wimpy" Favorite: "I hope."

I hope. Wimps love to pepper their presentations with this one. Why? ...Because they're afraid someone on the committee might not like them – even though they've never met these people and have no idea what they're thinking.

While they're at it, wimps weave this one in and out of everyday conversation, leading them into all sorts of wimpy, half-hearted relationships.

They tend to say, "I hope you like what I'm about to say," which **shouts insecurity**.

They might as well say, *"You probably won't like it, but I hope you like it anyway."*

Good grief, WHAT IS THAT? Exactly what are they saying?

**Why not complete the picture and wring your hands, whining, "Oh, I *hope* you enjoy this, I *hope* you'll maybe get something out of this, but you probably won't, so it's okay to tune me out."**

The phrase "I think" is equally as damaging to your image. Just listen: "I think we can meet your schedule." or "I think your project can be done for that budget."

At this point, some of us are beginning to wonder why we're sitting in the audience, listening to a wimp. No one is going to hire a firm that "thinks" they can do it. They are going to hire the team that "KNOWS" they can do it!

Repeat after me:

## *"NO WIMPY WORDS! BUILD TRUST. TELL YOUR CLIENT WHAT YOU WILL DO!"*

It might take practice for some people to exorcize "wimpy words" from their vocabulary. Start now. Just try it.

- *Record yourself in conversation.*

- *Listen to how you sound.*

Are any of the following "wimpy" words a recurring part of the way you present yourself?

### The Gallery of Notorious Wimpy-isms:

Do you routinely use any of the following in conversation?

**"Try"**

**"Hopefully"**

**"Maybe"**

**"Might"**

**"Probably"**

**"I think"**

**"I believe"**

**"In my *opinion*"**

## If you do, just STOP it! Stop right now!

Keep score. See if you can get through the day without resorting to Wimpy-isms.

If you use these Affirmations of Wimpy-ness in normal conversation, they're all over your presentation style. Again, cut it out!

Focus on the following...

## Positive Affirmation Words:

**Challenge.**

**We do it.**

**We are confident.**

**I know.**

Now, let's apply them to a sentence: **"We are confident. We do this."** Did you notice a phrase that was missing? "We will." Many of you say this – "We will develop a plan... We will do this; we will do that..."
So, what is wrong with that? As you use this phrase it becomes over-used and you develop a case of the wee-wees... and you are not in the moment. You lose your persuasiveness and conviction. It's simply more powerful to simply state what you do. Not what you will do.

## *Instead of saying we "will" do this, stand up and say, "We DO this."*

## Advance Affirmation

**When you walk into that interview, you want to act like you already have the job.**

**You're in the moment. You're solving their challenges. You're the best team.**

In your mind's eye, you're already moving forward and building that project.

***Don't say, "We will have a site specific safety plan."***

You want to say:

**"We HAVE a plan."**

**"We DO this."**

**"We DO this on every job."**

**"We do a Three-Week, Look-Ahead Schedule."**

You get the picture.....

## Be "In the Moment"

The simple state of just being in the moment, using **strong, positive words**, pulling out the subtle hesitations – the implied negatives – gives that client a sense of confidence...in you and in what you have to say.

*When your teammates drift into wimpy words, you have my permission to...*

**Throw something!**

**Hit 'em with a Nerf® ball!**

# Stand up, wave your arms, and shout:

# "NO WIMPY WORDS!!"

## The Cure

My husband spent his high school years in Houston. When he escaped and came to the Colorado School of Mines to go to college, he wanted to stop saying things like "y'all."

So, he had his college fraternity brothers hit him every time he said things like that, which cured him very quickly.

## Be a Wimpy-Word Watchdog!

**When you hear wimpy words, do whatever it takes. Cure your teammates of using them again, because they create doubt in the owner's mind.**

# As for YOU...

## *Banish Your Inner Wimp or...*

## *Get Off the Stage and Go Home!*

We've covered words. We have changed the way you listen for positive indicators in the way you stand up and talk.

Now, let's forget about words altogether. Good presenters know that it is the delivery of those words that tip the scales and create the winning presentation.

**The very SOUND AND TONE of your voice evokes PASSION** (or not).
Words do not evoke passion; words give information.

You can say in a monotone (note wimpy type-size): "Good afternoon I'm so excited to be here. Sincerely, on behalf of all of us, I hope you, maybe, like what I'm going to say, anyway, we are the right team for your project..." See how small it looks and feels in monotone-mode?

Sure, the words are there, but the way you sound is completely devoid of meaning. Who would believe you?

**Do NOT sound monotone. Use your voice to convey energy, excitement, and passion.**

It's all about the way you use your voice. It's all about how you deliver those words.

**Apply vocal dynamics because:**

1. Vocal emphasis and inflection are two of the best ways to spark interest in your audience. This also works in normal conversation.
2. Using inflection will emphasize key words in a sentence.
3. Fluctuating between louder and softer assertions keeps the audience listening and focused.

*How do you use your voice to further convey passion?*

This is an especially important question for people who talk a mile-a-minute.

- Remember to **PAUSE**, especially if you're a fast talker.

- Emphasize with silence your important comments.

- Using transitions will let your audience keep pace with you.

- If you feel like rushing in practice to get it all in, you have **too many words**: BOIL IT DOWN.

- Don't rush. Say less and say it with power and conviction!

This can be difficult for the chronically nervous among us but it's vital: Let your audience catch up with you.

*Remember to PAUSE for emphasis. Rushing through a*

# *presentation can sound just as canned as a monotone delivery.*

**Speak loud enough for everyone to hear you. They can't believe what they can't hear!**

This stuff is so important that here's a quick summary. Jot it down and save it for reference:

1. **Be aware of vocal tone and inflection.**
2. **Use variance in your speech.**
3. **If you speak fast, slow down.**
4. **If you're slow, pick it up.**
5. **Use a dramatic pause now and then.**

### Dying on the Stage

Visualize a doctor's electronic heart rate monitor, the one with the blipping screen and the line going up and down. This shows your heart rate.

**What does it mean if the line runs flat across the bottom of the screen? That's right: YOU'RE DEAD. Talk at the same, flat rate, without inflection and your presentation dies, too.**

You will put your audience to sleep. Instantly!

In short, you are going to die.

I once had a new firm call me. They had just lost the interview and the selection committee commented that it felt like they had just come from a funeral. The team lacked all emotion during the presentation and was monotone throughout.

# *Use your voice to convey passion. Your audience will stay interested by the virtue of HOW YOU SOUND.*

If you speak in a monotone, the attention span of your audience will flatline. You and your presentation will drop dead. ...Immediately.

The art of *sounding* confident vs. actually *having* confidence: This can be a tall order to begin with if you lack confidence when presenting. Let's work on that.

How many of us get a little nervous before an interview? Of course, you do. This is not what you are comfortable with; it's not your favorite thing to do. Well, don't worry; you're not alone. It's natural; we all fall into it. Most of us probably have a touch of "glossophobia" - the fear of speaking in public.

In fact, studies estimated that as many as 75% of all people experience some degree of anxiety or nervousness when speaking in public.

Actually, **a little bit of nervousness can be a good thing, too.**

If you **don't get nervous before a presentation, you might be flatlining.**

**You can use that nervous energy and turn it into the passion and excitement we are looking for.** Just make sure that nervous energy doesn't take control and become a negative.

## The Pep Talk

Here's one thing that can help a case of the "Nervous Nellies." Remember, you are the expert and you can help them.
Give yourself the following pep talk:

- **They need you.**

- **Your company believes in you.**

- **You are the expert.**

- **They are anxious to learn how you can help them.**

Every time I use my pep talk, it brings a smile to my face. It reminds me to relax and have fun with what I'm doing and that people will listen and enjoy what I am saying.

*Saturday Night Live*® fans have probably heard a certain character chant this one*: "I'm good enough. I'm smart enough. And, gosh-darn it, people like me!"*

Well, yes, you are and, yes, they do!

Those are the kinds of things I've learned to say to myself that have helped calm me down and give me confidence. You can use this one or make up one that works for you. But, do find a pep talk that works for you!

Going way back to my early days as a Dale Carnegie® instructor, we used to say: "All it takes is a little smile. Go ahead and force it if you have to. Utter a few positive words, just enough to take the edge off."

**I have a friend – a high-level executive with a lot of responsibility – who pretends to jam along to big-hair, heavy metal music on the way to the interview.**

Hey, I won't judge; whatever it takes, just do it. In your pep talk, you need to use all positive words. Some people are stuck with the opposite effect. Before going into the interview, they grit their teeth and mutter, *"Oh, I hate interviews. I'm no good at this. Why is it me they always have to drag along?"*

# *Develop a PEP talk filled with positive words!*

**You have earned the right to do this.**

**People want to hear what you have to say.**

**Go for it. Do it. BE it.**

# *Channel Your Inner Rock Star!*

# Do whatever works to

# BE CONFIDENT.

## Visualize

Other ways to rid ourselves of stress involve mental and visual outlets. Along with all-positive words in your pep talk, you can also use mental visualization.

Athletes like Lindsey Vonn™ use this kind of technique to de-compress **before a ski race**.

I listened to her talk at an event last year and she described the way she visualizes, in advance, every turn on the course. After she visits the course, she will actually re-visualize that course from 20 to 100 times, in her mind, the day before the race. She visualizes how her body needs to be posed when coming out of one curve and hurtling through another.

We do it when **playing golf**, too, and I'm the worst. When we come up to a water hazard, I tell myself, "Oh, I'm a goner." So, I dig out my water ball and guess what happens? Sure, I hit it right into the water hole.

One of these days I'm going to take my own advice and chant, "Positive, Positive, Positive!" as I take out the best ball in the bag and say, "What water?"

*The mind is an incredible piece of machinery. It is going to do exactly what we visualize doing.*

I know: I should fill my mind with positive words and images having to do with hitting that ball, watching it soar over the water hazard and on to the green. You work on your presentation and I'll work on my golf game. Deal?

*Walking into that interview with positive visualization increases the likelihood of success... exponentially.*

**Visualize success** in your mind. See the client smiling, shaking hands with you and handing you the contract. Be positive.

Never visualize failure. STOP THAT! Concentrate on positive thoughts.

**Think:** *"I am the best person and we are the best team for this project. We want to work on this project. The owner is interested in hearing how I'll approach this job. He wants me to get this project open for them."*

Fortunately, you can physically practice your presentation almost anywhere. Do it. This is a great technique when you are about to walk in and start.

**Mental Preparedness & Visualization**

*Take a moment and write down your own pep talk below:*

*After you have written out your pep talk (above)* confidence will come from being prepared, same as always.

Have you studied the client? Have you read everything you can find?

Prepping for a presentation is no different than prepping for any race or athletic event. We train, we put in the miles, we eat right, and we get our bodies in the best shape possible.

# *Preparation through mental preparedness is the foundation of confidence.*

## Mental Preparedness = Confidence

The more you have in your head about the project and the owner's vision...the more you've thought about how you plan to design or build the project...the more prepared and confident you will be.

Research. Practice. Create confidence through preparation.

## Physical Self-Therapy

The rest is about stretching, moving around, getting ready for the interview.

Think of how athletes always do their warm-up exercises before a game. The same thing applies before an interview. Warm up. Get some exercise in the morning. It doesn't have to be long or strenuous, just enough to get your blood moving. Try just a fast, 20-minute walk.

***Did you know that a simple, 20-minute walk will have a lasting, 12-hour effect on your nerves?***

Other little techniques include simple deep-breathing exercises, yoga, meditation, stretching or just tightening and releasing muscles, which increases testosterone, which will increase confidence. It, also will decrease the stress hormone known as cortisol. When you can balance the two and move their levels farther apart in your metabolism, the more success you will have with your nerves.

And exercise will increase your oxygen level. Once we increase the oxygen flow in the brain, we think faster and more clearly.

When a client puts you on their short list, it means they believe you are qualified to do the project. Now they want to get to know you. They want to know what it will be like to work with you. That's why they invited you to the interview. Remember, they've already seen your detailed RFP full of charts, budgets, schedules, etc.

.

1.  **They want to know how you will treat them on the job.**
2.  **They want to know how you work when issues come up.**
3.  **They want to know how you handle conflict.**
4.  **They want to get to know you and your values.**
5.  **They want to see how you solve problems and communicate issues.**

So, never try to be someone you are not.
Don't try to stand up and perform.
Just be yourself.

Remember the client who said, "We felt more comfortable with the winning team?" It was because the team members were honest and sincere, and they let the clients know what they were really all about.

They showed they are problem-solvers and good communicators who are looking out for the best interest of the client!

# *They don't want an actor, they don't want a game-show host...they want you to be who you ARE.*

**Make a mental transition** from being in front of a group - in a presentation conference room - **to sitting in a lively café**, enjoying the same conversation.

**Imagine being there**, in just such a place during the interview. Talk to your audience...almost **as if you were sitting down over lunch**, discussing them and their needs.

You would never read from a script in that situation, would you? Of course not. You might bring with you a list of bullet points to emphasize, but, you would never try to memorize even a short speech or conversation. How silly! Not with someone sitting directly across the table, looking into your eyes for meaning. It just won't work. You will most certainly forget what you want to say.

# *Engage your audience by having a* conversation *with THEM, about THEM.*

- When you do, remember you are the expert.

- Remind yourself that you are there to help them; that you have something to offer.

- Change your thinking: You are not there to "sell" and take away something from them.

- You have something they want; you are there to share.

It's just a different way of looking at the same thing.

# *People remember people who talk about them...not themselves.*

How many times have you been stuck in conversation at a party with some self-absorbed windbag who talks non-stop about himself? Before you have a chance to say a word about yourself, he's moving on to talk at someone else.

How do you feel about that individual? Annoying, isn't he? You certainly don't want to be remembered for that!

**Being pleasantly "memorable" means sharing stories that add value for the listener.** You can do this with short, to-the-point stories that show the client how you have solved similar challenges on other projects - projects similar to theirs, challenges similar to what they face.

Just make sure to **keep your stories informative and to-the-point**.

People remember stories, especially when well-told and related to them.

Using this simple technique, they will take away a more lasting memory of your story, especially if you engage them in conversation about what you just said.

Best of all, these simple methods will improve your business *and* personal relationships, wherever you go!

We've touched on preliminaries of being interesting, but now we can see that interesting and being memorable go together, don't they?

**The art of being interesting simply goes back to talking about *them*, who they are, what their business is all about and how it relates to their project.**

A few years ago, while sitting on the selection committee for an addition project at my church, I watched a first-hand example of how to lose a project – even when you happen to be the front-runner.

After reviewing and scoring the RFPs, we ranked the firms and invited the top three architects to come in and interview with our committee.

One firm stood above the rest, impressed us all, and we could hardly wait to interview them. After all, they had the largest, most impressive showing of church projects and we were flattered they would even want to do our little project.

## How NOT to be Interesting

Unbelievably, not long into the interview they were rambling on and on about all their other projects – to the point that it seemed like they couldn't care less about us. At one point, we even complimented them on their portfolio and *asked them to move on* in their presentation.

They didn't listen! They stuck to their slide show presentation as rehearsed and finished.

We couldn't believe it. Our previous #1 pick suddenly plunged to the bottom of the list. They did not win the job. Surprised? Not if you've been reading this book.

## Dog-and-Pony Shows are Not Interesting!

The biggest trend we see in presentations is the amount of prep time teams spend getting ready for the interview. The smart teams really dig in and learn as much as possible about the client, in advance. They know they MUST understand project challenges and present possible solutions, along with ways to overcome those challenges.

## Cut the Fluff

The art of being interesting also means you need to **cut out industry jargon, generic "on-time" and "on-budget" references, techno-fluff and chit-chat. Get to the meat of the topic.**

If a point is worth mentioning, make it specific to their project and what it means to them; otherwise, *lose it.*

Instead of making generic statements such as, "We will complete your project on schedule." Say something specific such as, "Prefabbing the headwalls allows us to complete your new Prairie View hospital by July 1st."

Using the name of their project and the actual dates makes the statement more interesting and makes a stronger, more trustworthy connection.

Once again, **people are always interested in themselves and the hurdles they face**, especially when it comes to something as arduous and challenging (in their minds) as a construction project.

# *Just make sure it's all about them and you will Be Interesting.*

**Look 'em in the eye** and be proud of who you are and how you can help them.

**Make eye contact.**

**Actually lock eyes with someone for a couple of seconds.** This creates a genuine connection. And, make it a habit to make a connection with everyone on the selection committee!

*Scanning is not eye contact!*

Scanning is what we do to assess a situation. We do this to take note of our surroundings and it indicates a state of warriness, such as when we walk to our car at night.

**Never scan the room if you are the speaker.**

Eye contact builds trust; if you never look at your audience, they aren't going to trust you and they certainly won't ever select you.

# *Build trustworthy connection*
# *with*
# *EYE CONTACT.*

**Finally, I want you to always…**

# *Practice, practice, practice: There is no substitute for being prepared.*

Being truly prepared will increase your confidence and help settle your nerves because you know your stuff.

That really is what it's all about.

*A three-session practice policy should be your Presentation Golden Rule.* Here's why: The first time you get together - especially superintendents and more technical people - you need time to digest information and sleep on it. In order to understand the project and get your arms around it so you can be comfortable talking about it.

I'm saying, talk it all out in advance and you know what I mean:

What exactly is the project? How will it be used?

Where is it? What are the logistical concerns?
What are the risks?
What are the challenges?
How do we go after solutions?

The more you can have that discussion with your team - the more you get all the ins-and-outs of that project on the table - the more confidence you will have because you understand that project.

# *Don't short change the time you need to process all this information.*

You will gain much more confidence sleeping on that information, as opposed to going straight into the interview. So many questions and solutions come up overnight as you turn the specifications and challenges over in your mind.

- Give yourself down-time to simply process that information.

- Then, go back and get into another practice session.

- When the third session rolls around you should also be practicing your part as well as possible questions and answers.

*The selection committee puts even more weight on the Q&A section! Be prepared for those tough questions.*

## The Dreaded "I Can Wing It" Syndrome

Now, let's talk about the free-wheeling few who always seem to think they can...Wing It.

I've been in this business a long time. I've ridden the cycle enough myself. Trust me. Rule Number One:

**Don't wing it.**
**Don't go there.**
**Don't risk it.**

Unless you've been nailing every presentation since you began your career, my guess is that you can't "wing it" for long and stay in business.

**We can get away with winging the old dog-and-pony show, but the old D-and-P is not going to win!**

**We can go on about the tired old company history and all the great things we've done...none of which have anything to do with the client.**

**What you can't "wing" is how to connect all that to your client.**

# *NEVER, EVER, EVER*

# "WING IT"

**Okay, we know we can't just wing it when addressing client issues and what they mean to the client and how we are going to solve those issues. Those issues really must be practiced and rehearsed – but NOT memorized.**

And you owe it to your teammates to practice so they feel more comfortable with the presentation as well.

Why not memorize the presentation?

## *Why Not MEMORIZE?*

For those who think rote memory is the way to go, please be advised:

## *Mr. Monotone Has Left the Building.*

- If it's scripted, it will sound scripted.

- If you try to memorize a script, unless you're some kind of Shakespearean actor, the client will pick up on it every time. And, if the client asks a question in the middle, you've now lost your place and can't get started again.

- Scripted sounds canned.

- Canned sounds indifferent and insincere.

*Make it easier on yourself – Don't memorize your part! Practice your part in a conversational manner. Know the key message you want to deliver.*

You actually put more stress on yourself when you try to memorize because, when you do forget a word – and you will – or if you get a little bit off track, you will become so nervous that you will usually lose the whole thing. And, you cannot recover from that.

You never want to try to memorize. None of us have that much time in our day.

- **Know your opening statement.**

- **Write out your bullet points.**

- **Have your bullets down.**

- **Talk naturally about each bullet point.**

- **Have your closing statement – so you know you are done.**

# *Then you will be conversational.*

### *PRACTICE OUT LOUD!*

So, why do we want to practice our talking points, out loud, in front of others during practice sessions?

Simple:

**What you hear in your head will be perfect.**

Have you ever practiced anything in your head, from a speech to song lyrics? It always sounds great, doesn't it? The words flow without a hitch, all perfectly formed without a single "uhm" or awkward pause, no wimpy words or "loss for words." In other words:

You sound like a Hollywood actor turned rock star. But try it again, out loud. It sounds a lot different, doesn't it?

*It is absolutely critical to practice talking through your bullet points, out loud, even before you practice in front of your team.*

### Listen to Yourself

Here's another technique: **Use voice recording on your own phone**. Talk to yourself while the recorder is running and play it back. Listen to yourself and keep trying. You will discover all sorts of things, from sounding flat and monotone to garbled diction to plain old vocal stumbling.

- Listen for the emphasis or lack of it.
- Try a little tonal variation.
- Try a pause here and there.

**Now, try it in the mirror.** Watch your own facial expressions. Do you look grumpy or approachable? Do you look friendly and likeable, but, insincere? Do you have good posture?

# Stand up *and* practice out loud!

## *Be Evolutionary!*

*You ARE evolutionary. You sensed a problem with the fading appeal of the old dog-and-pony traditional interview style.*

*So, you read this book. Maybe you took notes. It doesn't matter because you have already evolved. You took the time to read this book and consider my winning concepts, and they HAVE been winning interviews for people everywhere in our industry.*

*Now you have them in a portable form of instant reference, which can be taken anywhere in the world – no batteries needed!*

*Like I said in the beginning, mark it up, tear it out, and just take it with you. If you do, you will be absolutely evolutionary when you walk into your next interview. Your next client will love you for liberating them from another monotone canned presentation.*

*They will truly appreciate you for focusing on them and their concerns.*

*But remember: Nothing's in the bag, never, not ever. So, never try to wing it and know that being all the "BE's" in this book will take practice. But, please make no mistake: You already are a "winner" because you have dared to...*

## *BE!*

# FAQS

There are no perfect answers for the following questions but I've heard them all many times, with many variations on a theme. For now, let's go with a few stock answers, knowing that every owner, every committee, and every project will pose a different set of variables, right?

We see different issues and challenges every time, so what works in one situation, may not work in another. Always take into consideration what you know about your listeners and their needs. Just use the following for basic guidelines and, if things get tough, you know where to find me. My contact information is included on the last page of the book.

That said, the following are Frequently Asked Questions posed by people in our industry.

## Do we have the selection committee introduce themselves?

This one's easy: Absolutely!

How can you present to a group you don't know?

At the very start of the interview, and before the clock starts, ask the committee to introduce themselves. Have each one briefly identify **their role** on the project and voice any concerns they would like to have addressed.

Now, you can call them by name and direct meaningful issues to each person during your presentation.

This also helps engage interaction and gets them talking.

## How many of our people do we take to the presentation?

This one's easy when the selection committee dictates the number. It's more difficult when the owner leaves it up to you; here are some thoughts to help you determine who goes:

1. Always take key individuals with day-to-day responsibility on the project.
2. Take key individuals who differentiate your team.
3. Take people who have relationships with committee members.
4. Take people who provide added value. Yes, it is OK not to have everyone speak during a presentation and still bring them for the Q&A. (The time limits for formal presentations are getting shorter and the time allotted for Q&A is getting longer. Don't dilute your short presentation by having everyone speak.)

For example, a design team can include a sub-consultant known by the client, but always coach this sub-consultant. Have her talk about why she appreciates working with your team and how your project approach is beneficial.

And if this particular owner is a stickler for safety, bring along your safety director – showing that safety is equally important to you as well.

*When the selection committee limits your number of attendees*, I'll often send the executive or president to merely shake hands and give the corporate commitment during the set-up. After that, they excuse themselves and wait in the hall.

*Sometimes, they're invited to stay* and it makes a positive impression to show project commitment with executive presence. But, they should remain in the background and never have a large speaking role.

## Do we take the president or another exec?

Most often, yes. However, make sure they DO NOT overtake the presentation and do all of the talking. Their minimal presence is solely to support the team and show that the owner/client is important enough for the president to be present.

## How do we introduce team members who are new to our company?

It's best, of course, when the team has worked together and has a history on similar projects, which adds a level of comfort for the client.

However, if some team members are new to the company, sell their unique contribution to the team.

"Tom, our new PM, recently joined the company because the medical industry is an important market for us and we're constantly looking to grow our staff in this area."

Explain that "we jumped at the chance to bring Tom on board" due to his XYZ experience, adding strategic range and experience to the team.

Sell your benefits and strengths.

## Do we stand or sit?

This depends on the selection committee. Are they formal or informal? You can often tell by the physical setting of the room.

A small group may be looking for a "partner" and would be put off by flashy "fast talkers." In this case, it makes sense to informally sit around a table to make them feel comfortable and relaxed.

Your allotted time is another indicator. If you find yourself in a two-hour "work session," it is most appropriate for everyone to sit.

Primarily, you still want to strategically position your team members and have your PM centered for direct client contact. Again, seat your executives off to the side, helping to ensure that they won't take over and run the show.

*The shorter and more formal the presentation, the more appropriate it would be for your team to stand for the entire interview:*

*You don't want your team to look like a "Whack – A –Mole" game with people continuously popping up and down.*

## Should we use PowerPoint?

I hear this one all the time. The short answer: Place the utmost priority on the development and understanding of your key messages and content.

Then decide how you wish to present it: Is it Prezi®? Boards? Banner? or PowerPoint? But, don't let the visuals determine content!

When your slide show is crafted before the message is fully developed, the message becomes bogged down in speaker notes and bullet points, which are not visual!

Any visual - projected on a screen, TV or smart board - is not bad. More often, it is simply used badly.

Work with your team to ensure their knowledge of visuals and how to use them. Also, have them practice standing off to one side while maintaining eye contact and an open body stance with the selection panel.

And never let anyone turn their back on the committee.

We've been seeing a trend toward the use of animation and 3D modeling, which is here to stay. But, mainly, we're seeing teams spend more and more money and time on interview preparation to really understand the risks and challenges of the project and develop potential solutions to mitigate that risk.

## Should we include handouts?

If you have some sort of leave-behind/handout, make sure it's appropriate. A print-out of your slides is not appropriate.

Consider distributing handouts when appropriate during the presentation. Distribute handouts too early and people become distracted, flipping through them as you talk and losing track of your presentation.

Most teams go with a simple "placemat" that has pictures of the team and a simple, line-item agenda – so the selection committee can see upcoming topics, key differentiators or team benefits – along with white space for note taking.

## They have given us a list of questions. Do we have to follow them as an outline?

Yes and no. Yes, you need to answer all of their questions. No, you do not have to follow them in any particular order nor must they be addressed verbally. The important thing is make a connection with the folks on the other side of the table and deliver an engaging, easy-to-follow presentation with impact.

As you go through your presentation, make sure to point out when you are answering a question.

You can fully address all the questions in a written format and leave it for the committee to review after the presentation.

## What should I wear?

Recall my earlier story about the presentation before a rural selection committee and the team that appeared in suits and red power ties? The team went down in flames, of course.

On the flip-side of the equation, just before an interview our superintendent showed up wearing a T-shirt – YEP, a "round neck" – and, worse, it even looked more like a T-shirt you'd wear underneath another shirt.

The only redeeming quality of that T-shirt was its solid color and lack of writing or graphics.

Either way, we were on in 5 minutes and had no time to find him a new shirt and - needless to say - we lost. We looked too casual, showing a lack of respect for the owner. They felt we wouldn't take the job seriously - that, for us, it was "too small" to matter.

First impressions are important. Learn more about your client to make sure your team is sending the right message when they walk in the door. A simple rule of thumb is to dress a "step-above" your audience, thus showing respect but, not out-of-place or over-dressed. Always pay attention to the little details – polished shoes, well-pressed shirt and a belt. Women, stay away from lots of patterns and too much jewelry that can cause a distraction.

## Where do I look when one of my team members is presenting?

Just because you aren't speaking doesn't mean you're not "ON."

You are definitely ON at all times, from the moment you walk in the room until the moment you leave.

You might even be ON before you enter the room, from the moment you park and walk into the building. Maybe they can see you leave your car from the conference room and you never know who you might run into in the foyer.

When a teammate is speaking, your attention should be split equally between that speaker – nodding in agreement and showing positive support - and keeping a connection with the selection committee.

# I seem to say "UM" or "like" a lot. How do I break that habit?

The first step is to know you do it.

Have a co-worker raise their hand every time you say, "UM," or whatever your problem-filler may be. Once you begin to hear yourself say it, you can break it...the habit, I mean.

When you feel yourself ready to utter that dreadful word, take a breath, say nothing, and continue, leaving the word behind, unsaid.

When people are prepared, when they have practiced out loud, they have less of a tendency to let those unsightly filler words slip out.

# What do I do when I don't know the answer?

Listen to, and answer, questions to the best of your ability, but if you lack an immediate answer, never try to "wing it." *And NEVER, EVER LIE.*

**Just look them in the eye and say, "Let me check into that and I'll get back to you with the correct facts – I would hate to give you bad information."**

Write down their name, their unanswered question, and get a contact phone/email/business card. Then, do it.

Make a friendly "personal contract" with them to deliver their answer within a specific period of time, say 24 hours. Rarely, does such a specific question come about that you don't have any response.

## What do I do with my hands?

USE THEM!!

Unless you're a professional speaker, you will probably find it incredibly difficult to keep your hands in a natural resting position at the sides of our body.

Once there, it gets worse for most of us: Our sidelined hands turn into FLIPPERS from the wrist down. We start looking like fish out of water – fighting to get back to sea.

Practice having your arms and hands to your sides when walking a jobsite or talking to co-workers; this becomes more comfortable with time but most of us need practice. It isn't easy.

In the meantime, keep your arms above your waist and gesture when appropriate. It is easier to use your hands when they are already at your mid-section. Make sure your arms have structure and aren't loose and floppy; get your elbows unstuck from your sides.

It may be uncomfortable at first, but, you will look natural. Go ahead: Video yourself and you will see what I'm talking about.

If you are so incredibly uncomfortable that you physically shake, go ahead and put one hand in your pocket – making sure you have nothing in that pocket and that your slacks are loose enough for your hand to fit. This leaves your remaining hand for gestures. In time, you will feel comfortable enough to free your other hand and use it as well.

I'm one of the few coaches to say this is OK. I've seen it work and I'm a firm believer in taking small steps to achieve a comfort level. Feel free to do just that, then, of course, just...

Be Yourself, Conversational, Memorable, Positive, Confident, Passionate, Interesting, Prepared, Trustworthy, AND...

## *BE Evolutionary!*

# MY HEARTFELT THANKS

## ....to the Gifted and Dedicated Builders of the World

Thank you for reading my book of tips and tricks of the trade.

I wrote it specifically for the talented people in our industry who have found themselves – or who will eventually find themselves – facing the final step of the selection process, the short list presentation.

I've unloaded a conceptual truck load of tips and information in this book, which may take time to digest, but, that's why it was designed for consumption in little bits and bytes. The book was also designed for last minute skimming and reminders, so use it as you see fit, but please do use it to lead your team to victory.

As I have said throughout this book, not everyone will be 100% comfortable with all things in every chapter. But I know you can run with more than a few nuggets, feel more comfortable and win: That's what I want for you!

Just take it all in, be willing to try new techniques, be willing to practice and be willing to be yourself when you get into that client interview.

And if you ever have any doubts, if you need additional coaching or maybe just a quick reminder or two, you know where to find me. My contact information follows.

After working with thousands of people, all that went into this book, and after my decades in this great industry, my real "take-away" is in the knowledge that many of my readers will move on to create the new skylines with great buildings and the roadways and bridges to take us there. That's what gives me goose bumps and the determination to continue to find new tips and tricks to help all of you get better.

I want to contribute to your success, whether it's from these pages or when we have the chance to meet.

Until then, it's all about building relationships, building trust, building the winning presentation and BEing who you are and what you do.

Now, let's get out there and WIN WORK!

Yours, very truly,

Dena L. Wyatt

# ABOUT DENA L. WYATT

## *"Evolving" and "Differentiating" Winning A/E/C Teams Since 1994*

Dena Wyatt has been a major presence in professional marketing services for the construction-design industry since 1994, working with top teams and individuals to transform critical client presentations into the end-game result: Winning more work.

Founder and Principal of Marketing Evolutions Inc., she understands the complex selection processes of design and construction from the traditional design-bid-build to complex Design- Build to P3s. Having worked extensively with A/E/C firms, Dena has been able to build her own, unique custom, in-house training, coaching and mentoring – "evolving" executive and technical staff throughout the Southwestern and Rocky Mountain regions into strategically coordinated, confident, and winning teams.

She is *the* acknowledged expert in this industry as it applies to differentiating a firm's brand and product from its competitors.

She urges her clients to "Be Evolutionary" because marketing professional services in the construction design universe requires a quantum-evolutionary leap from "pushing widgets."

"YOU and YOUR PEOPLE are the brand, YOU are the product, and your work is the proof of who you are," Wyatt says. "Knowing how to transform and differentiate that message is the key to your success."

Her acclaimed workshops, keynotes, and partnering sessions have served nearly every regional top contender in the AIA, AGC, ACEC, SDA, CREW, NAWIC and SMPS.

Her techniques and strategies have re-written the rule book when it comes to presentation training and related insider perception surveys, which empower her teams and individual clients to achieve their objectives.

Dena is a past president, and a long-time director, of the Society for Professional Marketing Services (SMPS) Colorado Chapter, and is also a recipient of the Society's *Leonardo Award for Lifetime Achievement in Marketing Excellence.*

The success of her impressive list of grateful clientele speaks for itself.

## Contact Information

Dena L. Wyatt
Marketing Evolutions Inc.
999 18th Street, Ste 3000
Denver, CO 80222
dena@BEevolutionary.com
303-424-9462